Sowing Seeds of Purpose
(How to Harvest a Life Abundant)

Mary,

God Bless

Elliott West

Copyright © 2006 Elbert West
All rights reserved.
ISBN: 1-4196-4670-2
ISBN-13: 978-1419646706

Visit www.booksurge.com to order additional copies.

ELBERT WEST

SOWING SEEDS OF PURPOSE
(HOW TO HARVEST A LIFE ABUNDANT)

2006

Sowing Seeds of Purpose
(How to Harvest a Life Abundant)

CONTENTS

Introduction   xi

I. We're All Endless Bags of Seeds   1
   1. It's the President's Fault   3
   2. It's What You Believe That Matters   5
   3. If You Don't Like the View From the Back Seat, Get Up Front   7
   4. You Can't Sow Corn and Expect to Harvest Wheat   9
   5. "Sher' Hope Ya Like Them Ther' Cherry Tomatoes"   11
   6. Reaping Doesn't Happen Over Night   17
   7. Seed, Weed, Water and Wait   19
   8. Take It One Seed at a Time   21

II. Master of the Seed   25
   9. Spread It Around   28
   10. Giving with Purpose   28
   11. Practice Giving to Receive   32
   12. Be a Gracious Receiver   33
   13. Study a Master to Become a Master   34
   14. Flexing the Muscle of Universal Power   37
   15. Wanted: Someone to Apprentice a Master of the Seed   39

III. The 3 Universal Seeds of Power   45
  16. The Seed of Thought   46
  17. Practice Looking at Your Thoughts   53
  18. Don't Forget to Feed and Water   56
  19. Place Your Order with the Universe   56
  20. Share the Load   57
  21. The Seed of Word   58
  22. Speak or Don't Speak with Purpose   60
  23. Say What You Mean and Mean What You Say   62
  24. Aim Your Words Carefully   64
  25. Out with the Old, in with the New   65
  26. Develop a More Positive Vocabulary   66
  27. Your Words are a Magnet   70
  28. Words Can Cut Like a Knife   72
  29. The Seed of Action   75
  30. Keep Your Emotions in Check   76
  31. Desire   79
  32. Paint the Big Picture One Stroke at a Time   81
  33. Save Nothing for the Swim Back   85
  34. Actions + Purpose + Faith + Expectation = Success!   87
  35. Watch Out for the Weeds!   88

IV. Focus the Power of the Seed   91
  36. Feel the Power   92
  37. The Exact Factor   94
  38. Get to the Nitty-Gritty When It Comes to the Asking   97
  39. If You Don't Know What You Want or What You're Worth; Who Does?   100
  40. Why Learn From Your Mistakes When You Can Learn From Mine?   102

41. Jim Vaughn's Golden Rule	103
V. The When, Where and How to Sow	**109**
42. Sowing Seeds 3 x 7	110
43. Marriage (Sowing Seeds of Passion)	116
44. Your Other Relationships	136
45. Children	151
46. Walk a Mile in Your Child's Shoes	155
47. Health	174
48. Wealth	192
49. A Smaller Percentage of Something Is Better Than 100% of Nothing	194
50. Community	219
51. Get to Know the Gardener	233
52. My Eulogy by Others	235
53. This Is Who I Am Now	246
54. This Is Who I Want to Be	237
55. I'm Here Should You Need Me	238
56 Instructions for Life	239

INTRODUCTION

Like many of the master teachers that have come before me, I have read almost every personal-growth book that I could get my hands on over the past twenty years. Like a sponge with unquenchable thirst, I have absorbed the teachings of such masters as Anthony Robbins, Dale Carnegie, Zig Zigglar, Jack Canfield, Sarah Ban Breathnach, Joe Vitale and many others.

Having spent the past 18 years as a professional songwriter, I have experienced the uncontrollable burn to express my deepest love, pain and desires through song. I have experienced the glory of success in the form of the much sought after fame and fortune, having sold more that 7 million CDs worldwide. But I tell you there is no fire in the universe that burns hotter than the desire to share universal wisdom.

As I became more enlightened and in tune with my soul purpose, I realized that I had begun to gravitate toward teaching through public speaking and life coaching. When I could no longer contain the store of knowledge and truth I had absorbed, it became apparent to me that I no longer had a choice. I had to write. I was not inspired to express myself through song this time, but through *"Sowing Seeds of Purpose."* Before writing this book, I had to ponder the most appealing way of sharing my message with you. The universal answer was and is *simplicity*. So you can look forward to a simple, direct approach that is designed to inspire and motivate while providing you the necessary knowledge and tools to build a better *you*.

As a *life coach,* it has been my experience that while most of us have a lot of the same challenges, we each have different needs when addressing them. This book is designed to allow you to bounce around to the parts *you* feel are important at the very moment you are reading it. I have a tendency of doing this myself when reading works by other authors. My goal is to inspire you to live more consciously and to sow your seeds with *purpose*. Personal growth begins by your willingness to accept responsibility for all that comes to pass in your life. As long as you accept responsibility for all that directly affects you, whether it is good or bad, then you maintain the necessary control to influence whatever circumstances you wish.

You *can* have everything you want if you're willing to sow the seeds for a planned outcome. The important thing is that you have to want *success* more than anyone else in the world wants it for you! Thank you for allowing me the privilege of sharing your journey. May you harvest a lifetime of abundance.

I

WE'RE ALL ENDLESS BAGS OF SEEDS

You must take personal responsibility. You cannot change the circumstances, the seasons, or the wind, but you can change yourself.
JIM ROHN
Business philosopher

To help you get the most out of this book, I feel it is necessary to begin with a quick exercise. If you truly desire wisdom and personal growth, you must first be willing to accept responsibility for your existence and begin to understand to some degree, your impact on our universe. Yes, OUR universe. I call this affirmation the, *"I'm the king of MY world"* exercise and for your benefit, I suggest that you make it a habit of performing this exercise at the beginning of each day. By doing so, you will re-enforce and begin to embrace the first of what I call, *the universal laws of harvest.* There are ten laws throughout the book. Make a list of these laws and keep them close until they are branded into your memory. They will serve you well.

Law # 1: *Each of us is a constant and never-ending sower of seeds and is therefore responsible for the outcome of our harvest.*

Now, stand alone in the middle of the room with your arms and fingers fully extended straight out from each side of you. Pick a spot on the wall directly in your line of sight and slowly turn around until you come back to that focal point. This is *your* world and you're responsible for every thought you think from within it, every word you speak from within it, and every action you take from within it. Now, with that imaginary circle around you, walk to another room and stand in the center. Repeat the same exercise and notice how *your* world, along with every thought you think, every word you speak and every action you take follows you. Your life right now, is a direct result of all that has emanated from within this imaginary circle up to the very moment you are reading these words.

We are not victims of circumstances; we are not helpless products of our childhood or at the mercy of unseen dark forces. If our life stinks at this moment, this doesn't mean that God is punishing us for the sins of our past and it doesn't mean that we are not meant to have more or do better, it simply means that we could have, or should have made different choices. We are all spirits of freewill and are therefore responsible for the outcome of our lives. In other words, what you think, say and do today determines the outcome of your tomorrow.

> *My joy, my grief, my hope, my love, did all*
> *within this circle move!*
> Edmund Waller

Now, repeat this exercise and as you extend your arms and slowly turn, say out loud to your inner self;

"This is MY world. I have absolute control of all that happens within this space. I am responsible for every thought, every word and every action for I am the one who created them. Today and from now on, I will be conscious of every seed I sow."

Congratulations! You have consciously sown a very powerful seed in the most fertile soil of the universe, your subconscious mind. By making this exercise a morning ritual, you will affirm your accountability to yourself and the universe and assume absolute control of your destiny. From this day forward you are king of the world; *YOUR* world.

IT'S THE PRESIDENT'S FAULT

The reason I began this book with the previous exercise is to splash the proverbial cold water on your face. If you're not willing to accept 100% responsibility for your past, present and future, then close this book now and give it to someone who is. Being *king of your world* comes with a great deal of power in terms of the universe and with great power comes great responsibility (as said by Peter Parker's uncle Ben in the movie Spider-Man). We are more than willing to take credit and to be held in high regard when we achieve great things big and small in our lives, but we quickly cower into a posture of finger-pointing when things don't go well or when faced with failure. For the most part, it is human nature to do so.

We blame our parents and their inadequacies during our childhood for our failures as adults. We blame the President for the economy that hinders our ability to obtain the financial security we desire. We blame our friends, family and spouses for the lack of positive support that stifles our entrepreneurial spirit. We blame the weather, the fast food industry, the cigarette companies, the oil companies, the devil, God and even our ancestors. We blame everything and everybody but ourselves. The challenge with transferring the blame away from ourselves is that we also transfer the control to fix or change whatever doesn't meet with our satisfaction.

Remember, if you're obese, *you're* the one who ate unhealthy and failed to exercise regularly or to seek help from a medical expert. If you didn't follow through on your dream because of derogatory remarks from friends and family, then *you're* the one who gave up. How can you expect to get where you want to be in life if you don't have control over the vehicle taking you there? If someone else is at the wheel, then you are at their mercy. *They* decide in what direction you travel, the turns to take and the speed at which to get there.

If you blame McDonalds or the accessibility of fast food for your obesity, then you've basically put yourself at the mercy of McDonalds or other fast food chains to remedy the situation. When you allow the negative opinions of friends and family to stop you from realizing your dreams, it's *your* fault. By blaming them for your failure to succeed, you have given them control over your ability to attain success. If it's their fault you failed, then it's up to them to make it right. Honestly, do you really want to put your success in the hands of dream stealers and nay-sayers?

It would be an absolute blessing to have the unconditional support of others when reaching for our dreams, but it's not necessary. It's your dream and your happiness at stake, not theirs. Repeat after me; *"If it's to be, it's up to me."* Today, you have just realized that you are king of your world; all you have to do now is to accept this fact and take responsibility.

Another way to look at it would be the President of the United States. When we don't like inflation, immigration or the high price of gas, we simply blame the President. Now, we're all intelligent enough in this country today to realize that our President doesn't have absolute power to call all the shots. He shares responsibility for our country with the House and Senate and then there are the various state governments, but nonetheless, it's *his* job to take responsibility, good, bad or indifferent for all that affects our nation and we feel better having just one target to shoot at.

Just like the President, you too have to be willing to take responsibility for all that happens in your world, even when you feel the circumstances are beyond your control. Remember, it's *your* world and *you're* the President over all that resides within that imaginary circle we discussed earlier. *You're* the ruler over your every thought, word and action. Your world within the imaginary circle can be a barren desert or a beautiful luscious garden where your thoughts, words and actions can be the seeds which if sown with purpose, will bring forth harvest after harvest of abundance. These 3 seeds harness all of the power that exists in the universe and when you begin to truly hold yourself accountable for sowing them, it is then, that you will be able to exercise absolute control over the outcome of your harvest.

Understanding the power you possess as a universal *sower of seeds* and being willing to accept responsibility for your harvest is the first step. You have gained awareness, but before we can begin to seed your garden, we must first come to terms with your wants, needs and beliefs.

IT'S WHAT *YOU* BELIEVE THAT MATTERS

If you talk with a variety of individuals and ask two simple questions; *"What do you see in the mirror?"* And *"How do you view the world we live in?"* you would absolutely be amazed at the array of answers you receive. We tend to live up to whatever image of ourselves we believe to be true. For instance; if a person believes he or she always bounces back from life's down-turns, then you will find that they eventually do. If a person believes he or she is meant to serve a greater purpose in life than the average, then you will notice that they always seem to attract above average opportunities. If you believe you can, you can. If you believe you can't, you can't. If you believe you're a victim, then you're a victim. If you truly believe you are destined for great success in this life, you'll carry yourself with a suiting posture causing those around you to believe in your destined success as well.

You have as much control as you are willing to accept responsibility for, but how you see yourself and your world, does make a difference. The fact that you're reading this book tells me something about you. You either have already accepted responsibility for your life and this material is simply a form of reinforcement or you have just decided to take control and become accountable and this is your education. Really give some thought to how you view yourself and your own personal world. If you think your current beliefs and views might be a hindrance to your personal growth and success, then you're the king; change them. Understand that, if you keep doing what you've always done, then you're going to keep getting what you've always gotten.

You're probably thinking; *Change my beliefs and views!? He doesn't have a clue of how hard this is going to be for me!* I know it won't be easy. It rarely is. It just comes down to how important having successful relationships, successful children and/or financial success is to you. After all, you're not alone. We're in this together. We've started by taking responsibility. Now we're going to simply change our patterns of limitation so that we can begin to get exactly what we want. Up to this point you've most likely spent more time and energy complaining about what you *don't* want instead of purposely sowing the seeds that will allow you to harvest what you *do* want.

IF YOU DON'T LIKE THE VIEW FROM THE BACK SEAT, GET UP FRONT

If you limit your choices only to what seems possible or reasonable, you disconnect yourself from what you truly want, and all that is left is a compromise.
Robert Fritz
Author of *The Path of Least Resistance*

There are many metaphorical views of life and which metaphor you use as a reference will tell you a lot about yourself and how you deal with life's daily challenges. For instance; people who refer to life as a game, tend to handle challenges in a more strategic manner, garnering a "win some, lose some" attitude.

Those who refer to life as a big stage where they see themselves as simply playing a role, tend to have the ability of stepping back from a challenge the way an actor would, to critique their character in a play or movie. This helps to provide a third party view of their situation so they may then make whatever adjustments they deem necessary. Some see life as a journey for the purpose of spiritual growth and advancement, some see life as a war to be fought in a series of battles and then again, some see life as a bitch and then you die.

Ask yourself; *"what is **my** metaphorical view of life?"* I view life as a garden of boundless abundance and myself as a constant and never-ending sower of seeds.

My goal now is to help you to be conscious of each and every seed within you and to teach you a system for strategically sowing the ones that will bring forth the harvest you want. As you continue to read, give some thought to what area or areas of your life you want to improve. In other words, *what do you want?* You can't just complain about what you don't like or don't want, you must know *exactly* what you do want in order to even know what seeds to sow and where to sow them.

If you don't like your job, then decide what job you do want and go find it. Don't just stay where you're at and make everyone else miserable. I'm not saying that you have to quit abruptly and go broke while putting in applications, I'm just saying that you *do* have choices other than complaining about your current situation as if you're helpless. This is one of the areas of your garden that I have included specific instructions on seeding and weeding.

One day, my neighbor and I were engaged in a conversation about her dissatisfaction with her current financial situation. She explained how she and her husband were both unhappy with his job as it did not provide them quite enough money to live as comfortably as they would prefer. She went on for at least 35 minutes describing various financial challenges and how it would be nice if they could have their own business.

So, I finally asked, *"So, why doesn't he just find another job or maybe start a business of his own?"*

And she replied, *"Oh, he can't go into business for himself. He has a 401K and we just can't live without the health insurance."*

So, I simply said, *"What are you complaining about? It would seem that the two of you have made up your minds that you are without choices, so why not just make the best of your situation?"*

As you would imagine, this statement did not go over very well. She stood silent for a moment and made an excuse to exit our conversation.

The bottom line is, no one wants to stand by and listen to your constant complaining. If you don't like your current situation, decide what you *do* want and make a change. If you're not willing to make a change, simply keep your misery to yourself.

Now, if you *have* decided to change your current situation and you're willing to accept responsibility for the seeds you sow, then the first thing you must do is to decide *exactly* what you want.

YOU CAN'T SOW CORN AND EXPECT TO HARVEST WHEAT
For whatsoever a man soweth, that shall he also reap.
Galatians 6:7

We're all endless bags of seeds. The challenge for most of us as we move through this life, is that we carelessly and unconsciously sow seeds that have both a negative and positive impact on our lives. Since the majority of the world's population believes in some form or another that what we put out into the universe comes back to us, this leaves a lot of us confused or disappointed at the time of our harvest. We may have found ourselves with an abundance of corn when what we really wanted or expected was to harvest wheat. In other words, we may find ourselves in the middle of a nasty divorce when what we really wanted or expected was to be harvesting the bliss and contentment of a happy marriage with our soulmate. It comes down to one simple rule; know exactly what you wish to harvest, and then sow as many seeds as you possibly can toward that outcome.

Take care to avoid sowing any seed that will bring forth an unwanted harvest. If you don't want to harvest negativity, don't sow the seeds. If you wish to reap a more positive outcome, sow as many seeds as you can to ensure an abundance of that positive outcome. The more you sow, the more you grow. The question now is; what do you wish to reap?

Some examples of *negative seeds* would be: *Fear, self-pity, doubt, helplessness, condemnation, vulgarity, anger, regret, hate, arrogance, greed, false pride* and *addiction*.

Some examples of *positive seeds* would be: *Tithing, forgiveness, hope, love, mercy, encouragement* and *acceptance*.

Up to this point in your life you have had a pretty nasty habit of carelessly sowing a lot of negative seeds. Though you've also sown more positive seeds than you realize, I'm sure you would agree that the negative seeds seem to have a more noticeable impact than the positive ones. This is due to the fact that for the most part, we tend to concentrate more energy on the areas of our lives that are not working to our satisfaction and many times either take for granted or fail to celebrate the multitude of successes we deem too small to count.

A good example would be of a man who finds himself unhappy with his choice to drop out of school before graduating. He sowed a seed that would eventually limit his choices in life leading to a minimum wage job, his barely making ends meet, not much, if any nest egg and facing a meager retirement.

He may have a couple of healthy children, a beautiful wife that loves him and his own good health, but he chooses to be miserable over his lack of financial success instead of seeing how blessed he is for successfully sowing the seeds that grew a loving relationship with his wife, his children and his own good health.

It reminds me of the query, *"If a tree falls in the forest and no one is there to hear it, does it make a sound?"*

If you're expecting a harvest of blessings in your life, you have to actually see them as blessings. If you've ever grown cucumbers, then you have experienced the effort involved in harvesting them. Many times, due to the fact that the cucumbers blend so well with the leaves of the vine on which they grow, I've missed a few during the picking process only to discover them later being over-sized and not very palatable.

Make it a point to give the different areas of your life a little closer look and you might just find you have more blessings and successes than you thought. The good news is that you can affect the balance of your harvest. You are not helplessly tugged along this journey without choices.

The first step we must take together is to plug the leak-hole and develop the habit of sowing with a purpose or specific goal in mind. As I said before, you first have to decide what you want and when and why you want it.

"SHER' HOPE YA LIKE THEM THER' CHERRY TOMATOES"

Every year since my early twenties, no matter how busy my life is at the time, I've managed to have a little vegetable garden. Though I put a great deal of time and effort in *all* areas of my garden, I've always given special care to my tomatoes.

One year, I decided for the first time to plant cherry tomatoes. I stopped by a little roadside garden stand and purchased five little cherry tomato plants. The farmer asked if I had ever grown cherry tomatoes before and I told him I had not, but was looking forward to having some for my salads and eating some straight from the vine. He informed me that I probably wouldn't need any more than one or two plants as they were heavy producers, but I felt pretty sure I knew what I was doing, and therefore, decided to stay with my decision to buy the five plants. After all, I figured that what I couldn't eat, someone else would.

After paying for the plants, I thanked the gentleman for his advice and proceeded to my car. Just as I reached my car, the farmer made one last statement that I would later come to appreciate and find to hold a lot of wisdom.

He said, *"I sher' hope ya like them ther' cherry tomatoes."* I had no idea at the time just how much I would learn from the farmer's statement and those five little cherry tomato plants.

By summer's end, I found myself wishing I had asked the farmer what he meant by his last statement. He was right; I didn't need five plants. In fact, one would've been more than sufficient. The five little cherry tomato plants would later produce an over-abundance of fruit, but more than that, they and the farmer taught me one of the most valuable lessons I have ever learned.

As you would imagine, by the time autumn came, I was absolutely sick of cherry tomatoes and so was everyone else I knew. In fact, we were all so tired of the cherry tomatoes, that I had quit picking them well before the end of summer, allowing them to simply fall to the soil and rot. Much to my amazement, the plants continued to render little tomatoes well into the holiday season. I can't tell you how happy I was when the last plant finally succumbed to the cold. Little did I know, my lesson was not quite over yet.

The very next spring upon planting my new garden, I noticed some interesting weeds growing amongst the rows of plants. The cherry tomatoes were back. Evidently the rotting tomatoes from the previous season had left behind seeds that, due to a mild Tennessee winter, had not perished. I would spend the next two summers pulling small cherry tomato plants from my garden. It was then that I understood what the farmer had tried to tell me.

I shared my experience with the cherry tomatoes with you to make several valuable points. The first one being that any time you have a chance to avoid learning an unnecessary lesson, do so. The farmer tried to tell me from his own personal experience that I was planting considerably more than I needed. He didn't even bother to elaborate on his final remark as he could tell by my polite arrogance that I was unwilling to heed his advice. He decided I would eventually receive my lesson the hard way.

The second point and most valuable part of the lesson is, *make sure you really want and are willing to reap what you sow.* I knew I wanted the cherry tomatoes, but not *that* many of them. Had I listened to the farmer and researched the plants, I would've known how robust they were and could've lightened my load. This is one of the great lessons for all of us as *bags of seeds* to etch into our subconscious minds. Really do your homework and understand just what kind of harvest you're facing. Almost every plant, tree, flower, grass and yes, even weeds grow to spawn new seeds. It is the circle of life and just like the cherry tomato plant, many times we sow seeds that we may've thought we wanted to harvest only to later regret the choice and find ourselves with the spawning of new seeds leading us to harvest more of what we've decided we no longer want or need. Another great example of this would be my own recording career.

In the year 2000, after a decade of writing songs for other country music singers, I suddenly found myself with the opportunity to take the spotlight as a recording artist. It was a dream come true with one catch; the record label was looking for a singer with a bit of an outlaw image.

My producer at the time made me aware of this fact and though I already fit the description, I decided to really turn it up. I went on to record a CD full of *don't give a damn* attitude and filmed a video for CMT reflecting the same. I got what I thought I wanted, but I couldn't escape the raucous image I myself had created. I had sacrificed the freedom to show other sides of my artistic ability.

When I would look for new material, the Nashville songwriters would only send songs to fit the very image that had become a stone around my neck. Any time I had even the slightest confrontation with the label executives or the owner, it would be taken as a show of disrespect and a disregard for their position of authority and I would be punished in some way or another.

As you can see, I've had to learn this lesson the hard way. We will revisit this lesson using other examples throughout the book as it is one of the most important of the universal laws of harvest.

Law # 2: *Be sure you absolutely want, need and understand the magnitude of the harvest before you sow the seed.*

SOWING SEEDS OF PURPOSE (HOW TO HARVEST A LIFE ABUNDANT)

A journey of a thousand miles must begin with one step.
Ancient Chinese Proverb

During the early nineteen-nineties while I was experiencing my first success as a Country Music songwriter, I was approached by an uncle, who was a Ruby in the Amway organization at the time, with an opportunity to make a substantial residual income from the comfort of my own home. I was 27 years of age at the time and up to this point in my young life, had never before been exposed to multi-level or network marketing. My wife and I had just been blessed with the birth of our first of three little miracles and we both agreed that regardless of my newfound success as a songwriter, it would be nice to supplement one residual income with yet another.

As I said, I had never before been exposed to multi-level or network marketing, but as my uncle began to draw circles and recant the story of how McDonalds grew from one little restaurant to the many of current day, I became absolutely enamored with the idea of duplicating my efforts through the efforts of many. I was sold on the idea of building what my uncle called *the people's franchise*. My wife and I were 100% on board and anxious to join the ranks of the Amway elite; we were going to be Diamond Distributors.

We began to build our Amway franchise with the enthusiasm of a child in anticipation of Christmas morning. We went to the meetings and rallies, listened to the motivational tapes of our leaders on every road trip and went after every body with a pulse for the next two years. We didn't do too badly. In fact, we did really well for our first time participating in an MLM.

We eventually left Amway, but I was hooked and over the next 10 years, I would go on to participate in several other MLMs on my own. I never made the millions I had planned with the various network companies, but I was absolutely head-over-heels for the concept of the people's franchise and a believer still to this day. Where multi-level marketing is concerned, I gained much more than the millions of dollars, I had planned on generating through duplication, I had unknowingly learned how to sow seeds of purpose.

From the moment my wife and I became a part of Amway, our leaders would either give to us or suggest we purchase specific books to read such as, *See You at The Top*, *Think and Grow Rich*, *The Power of Positive Thinking*, *How To Win Friends and Influence People* and *Awaken The Giant Within*, to name a few. We would also subscribe to monthly tapes where various Amway leaders would motivate their down-lines through stories and positive affirmations.

This book is a perfect example of harvesting previously sown seeds. While I first believed that I had failed to attain what I deemed to be success in Amway and other similar companies, the seeds were being unconsciously sown that would lead to my current beliefs and the principals that I share with you in this book.

Although currently, I am not participating in a multi-level or network marketing venture, I will tell you that companies with such a structure are prime examples of sowing seeds of purpose. They teach you to duplicate your efforts by inviting others into your organization where you then teach them to do the same, all the while generating income not only from your individual efforts, but from a percentage of the efforts of others as well. What you're learning to do is to sow seeds that grow to spawn other seeds that in turn grow to spawn still other seeds, and so on. Everyone has a chance to enjoy an abundant harvest. Multi-level marketing companies use the principals in this book by teaching their members that *in order to get what you want, you must first help someone else get what they want.*

REAPING DOESN'T HAPPEN OVER NIGHT

Just as this book took 15 years after my experience with Amway to come into being, you need to understand that there is a time delay between the sowing and reaping. I had no idea at the time that the principals I was learning with multi-level marketing would lead to my reaping this book. Remember, when you sow the tomato seed, you don't begin picking tomatoes the next day, it takes time.

The good news is, whatever we sow, we will reap multiplied many times over. The bad news is, whatever we sow, we will reap multiplied many times over as well. Notice anything you would plant in your vegetable garden. When you plant one tiny tomato seed, do you harvest only one tomato? No, you may harvest as many as 30 to 40 and even as many as 100 tomatoes from that one seed. Remember the cherry tomatoes? You not only harvest in multiples, but *that* seed matures to spawn still other seeds that depending on *you*, may be sown with purpose or with carelessness. Let me explain. When the tomato seed has matured into a tomato plant, you will then harvest your tomatoes. You may also harvest some of the seeds from the tomato to sow at a later time. If you don't pick all the tomatoes, they will eventually fall to the ground and begin to rot, sowing their seeds without your help.

What do you want to reap abundantly? It's your choice. Now that you know the potential of reaping as much as 100 times what you've sown, what will it be? Will you sow anger or kindness? Will you sow greed or generosity? Will you sow pessimism or optimism? The most important question is; will you become more aware of what and how many seeds you are sowing? You've decided to take responsibility for each and every seed. You have a better understanding of how easily you can reap an over-abundance of what you don't want.

Now, we must begin to concentrate our efforts on helping you to sow your seeds with purpose. After all, you are an endless supply of seeds with free will. You can have anything you want and as much as you want of it. Have you decided what you want yet? Do you want a successful marriage? Do you want a successful career, a better job or a business of your own? Do you want happy, healthy, successful children? Maybe you would like to make a significant difference in your local community or better still, your world community. Maybe you want fame or maybe you just want physical and spiritual well-being. In the coming segments of this book I'm going to show you how to sow with purpose to help you achieve success in any or *all* of these areas of your life.

Now, let us focus on getting you into the habit of *consciously* sowing your seeds to get *exactly* what you want while helping you to avoid sowing the ones that will render what you *don't* want. Understand that some seeds will grow quickly, some will take time and some won't even break the soil. The important thing to remember is that you must sow excessively to better your chances of harvesting success in the areas of your garden that are important to you.

SEED, WEED, WATER AND WAIT

Here is where persistence and consistency will serve you well. Your marriage, your children (if you have any), your health and well-being, your career or business and your community make up what I call your *life-garden*. If you've never cared for a garden of any kind, just ask someone who has and they will tell you that it requires a lot of work and care. Just like my vegetable garden, I have found tending my life-garden to be a labor of love and you will too. It's like holding a lottery ticket and knowing that it is up you as to whether you win or not. The feeling you will have each morning when you wake up will be that of absolute excitement and anticipation toward seeding and tending your garden. You will know exactly what you're growing every step of the way and this will strengthen your expectation of success.

Have you ever bought a ticket for a powerball lottery when the jackpot is really big or been around someone who has? Do you recall the feeling of anticipation? It's amazing the feeling you get just planning all the ways the money will change your life. You allow yourself, if but for a day or an evening, the luxury of uninhibited dreaming. I've been there with the ticket safely tucked away in my wallet as though it were without a doubt *the big winner*. I've sat with my wife for hours the evening of the drawing planning to the detail every step we'd take when we found that we've actually won.

My wife and I would need an attorney, accountants and a couple of body guards to escort us to the lottery headquarters. We would plan who we'd help and how, where we'd live and all the wonderful dreams we could and would finally realize not only for ourselves, but for those we cared about. We would provide grants for the less fortunate. We would live off the interest. We would give to churches. The adrenaline would be pumping in anticipation and for a moment, for just a moment, we believed without a doubt the money was ours and all our dreams were about to come true. Can you imagine having this feeling every single day of your life? It would be euphoria.

If you will get up every day knowing exactly what you want to harvest, with a plan of what seeds you're going to sow and where you're going to sow them, you *can* have this feeling. You have to stay the course and practice patience. Get to your garden every day and sow in excess to ensure the desired harvest and truly expect to achieve it. It is important for you to understand that your follow-through is the key to your success. You sow what you want or need and then feed, water and weed. This doesn't mean that you sow a single seed and then stop and devote all your energy to that one. If you wish to ensure a successful harvest, you must sow as many of that particular seed as you can. For instance, if you like cucumbers, you don't want to depend on the survival of one single plant. To be safe, you must sow more of the same seed every day until you obtain the desired result.

Success is the sum of small efforts, repeated day in and day out.
Robert Collier
Author of *The Secret of the Ages*

When you continually re-enforce your future harvest by sowing additional seeds daily, all of a sudden you find yourself at ease with the universe. You realize that you absolutely *are* going to reap the success you desire. It's just common sense. If you consistently hit a brick wall with a sledge hammer enough times, it doesn't matter how big or thick the wall, it *will* come down. This is how some people have the ability of walking with a posture of absolute confidence. They know they are going to repeatedly sow the same seeds every single day in whatever area they desire success. In other words, if you consistently sow corn every day, you know that you are going to reap corn. Even if some of the seeds fall on unfertile soil, you *will* reap corn, because you've increased your odds by sowing so many. This fact will tend to give you a great deal of confidence.

Take Thomas Edison for an example. At the time of his death in 1931, he held 1,093 patents. Mr. Edison encouraged his productivity and phenomenal success by setting regular targets. Two of his targets included one minor invention every 10 days and one major invention every six months.

You see, Edison discovered early on, that thinking skills are greatly enhanced when put under pressure. This system, along with self-imposed pressure on his intellect, helped him reach his goals. You have to constantly re-enforce your seeding to ensure a successful harvest. The system I'm going to teach you will be similar to that of what Thomas Edison created for himself. The first thing we must do now is to become completely aware of our every thought, word and action so that we may begin to move forward with purpose.

Law # 3: *To ensure an abundant harvest, a seed must be sown and sown again until there is absolute certainty of the desired outcome.*

TAKE IT ONE SEED AT A TIME

Take the first step in faith. You don't have to see the whole staircase just take the first step.
Dr. Martin Luther King Jr.

When it comes to success of any kind, it's easier when broken down into individual steps. You have your 10-step programs and your 12-step programs, but I'm going to introduce you to a 3-step program. I have found that most people fail to reach their goals because they either experience burnout or they grow weary from participating in programs that require an excessive number of complex steps.

Most of us just don't have a lot of time that we can steal from our busy schedules for personal growth and enhancement. We prefer simplicity. It doesn't have to be complicated and drawn-out. You'll notice that even with this book I have made it a point to keep it short and easy to follow. I love reading more than anything, but if you're like me, then you don't have extended periods of quiet time to spend reading and feeding your mind. When it comes to personal growth, most of us prefer a book that can be read and absorbed over a 3 day weekend or at the most, over the course of a week.

My most important goal here is to make sure you receive, understand and can apply the information you need to help you *help yourself.* Throughout part I of the book you've had to come to terms with the fact that you are responsible for your every thought, word and action. You've had to come to terms with the fact that everything happening in your world at this moment is a direct result of seeds you have previously sown. Hopefully you have begun to understand the incredible power of the universe at your fingertips and how by sowing with purpose, you can absolutely harvest anything in life your heart desires. If you've already decided what it is you want, then you're ready for part II and beyond.

Understanding that all this universal power exists within you does you no good if you don't know how to make use of it and knowing what you want is equally useless without the tools to help you obtain it. From this point forward, you will learn to harness the power that resides in even the smallest of the seeds within you and become conscious of every single one that comes in contact with the proverbial soil of your garden.

II

MASTER OF THE SEED

You can be anything you want to be, if only you believe with sufficient conviction and act in accordance with your faith.
Napoleon Hill
Author of Think and Grow Rich

I'm not going to sugar-coat the task that lies before you and though what I am going to teach you is quite simple, the truth is, it's going to require commitment and effort. Most of all, this requires follow-through on *your* part. I learned a long time ago that, if you want to succeed or excel at anything in life, get near and study any individual or individuals that are already *where you want to be.*

I'll do my part to get you as close as I can to those that have gone before you sowing seeds of purpose. I will do this occasionally throughout the remainder of this book by providing you examples of individuals or groups of individuals that have become what I call *masters of the seed.*

To become a master of the seed, you must learn to *be the seed.* You must understand and accept that every seed you sow is an extension of you. I've always found a great deal of pleasure in reading success stories. I enjoy reading the stories of how other people overcome adversities to achieve success and greatness. This inspires me by helping me to understand that others have gone through many of the same struggles that I have and not only survived, but succeeded. I get to study their strategies and techniques for success and learn from their mistakes. Autobiographies of successful people provide a proven road map for the rest of us to follow.

Now that you are tuned-in to the sowing of the seed philosophy, look around; you will be amazed at the extraordinary impact other masters have had and are having by sowing consciously. One of my favorite stories is that of *Pierre Omidyar*; a true master of the seed.

Pierre invented the online auction site that became eBay, as a lark. But when his whim became a business that made him a billionaire, sudden wealth brought with it an overwhelming responsibility.

"There was this sense of 'Oh boy, what do we do to make sure that this wealth doesn't get wasted?" he says. *"We've got to put it to good use."*

From age 39, Pierre has devoted himself full time to the challenge of "responsibly investing" one of the dot-com era's largest fortunes, around $10 Billion. Pierre has since left eBay and abandoned Silicon Valley for a quieter life in Nevada, where he and his wife, Pam, started a family foundation. In 2004, they converted it into the Omidyar Network, a philanthropic venture-capital fund that, unlike traditional charities, can invest in profit making businesses as well as nonprofits. *"The recipients,"* says Omidyar, *"are chosen because they help people tap into their own power."*

That philosophy has put Pierre on the cutting edge of foundation work and created an eclectic portfolio of good works. Since 2004, the Omidyar Network has committed nearly $80 million to several dozen organizations. About half went to profit making ventures that create what Omidyar calls "deep social benefit." One is InnoCentive, a collaborative research community that allows pharmaceutical companies to post challenges to scientists around the world; another is World of Good, which imports the work of artisans in developing countries for sale by U.S. retailers.

The rest goes to nonprofits such as KaBOOM!, which organizes communities to build their own playgrounds, and Modest Needs, a group that channels small amounts of money to help poor working families who've been hit by unexpected expenses. Recipients of the gifts often become donors when they are back on their feet. Omidyar says his philanthropic approach is motivated by the lessons of eBay, which helped millions of ordinary people become entrepreneurs.

Omidyar's greatest passion is microfinance, the practice of making loans as small as $40 to entrepreneurs in developing countries. "It's not about alleviating poverty through charity," he says, "It's about giving someone the tools they need to make their own life successful, actually trusting them with something they might not have been allowed to touch before, which is money. He has given millions to the Grameen Bank, a leading private microfinance lender. "Business can be a force for good," he says. "You can make the world a better place *and* make money at the same time."

Pierre is a perfect example of sowing seeds of purpose. With $10 billion at his disposal, he would've unconsciously sown literally tens of billions of seeds anyway, but he chose instead, to be aware of what he sowed. By directing his wealth in a manner that actually helps people help themselves, he has created a never-ending reproduction of seeds. There is literally no way of calculating how many people will be blessed by the multitude of harvests as a direct or indirect result of seeds sown by Pierre. He truly *is* a master of the seed. Imagine what would've happened had he chosen to sow negativity.

SPREAD IT AROUND

Masters of the seed find a great deal of pleasure in sharing the fruits of their labor. Every year as I harvest my tomatoes, cucumbers, cabbage, corn, beans and so on; I share the produce I have raised with a great deal of pride and joy. After all, I can't possibly consume all that I have grown and besides, I am proud of my harvest and very much want others to enjoy it with me.

Remember, you will reap many times over, what you have sown and if you're sowing seeds of success in all areas of your life, you will have way more than any one person or family can enjoy alone. Understand that as you share from your life-garden, you are also passing along seeds that may be sown by others. In other words, when you give your neighbor a couple of tomatoes from your garden, inside those tomatoes are seeds that may be accessed by the beneficiary and sown if they choose to do so. You actually have a chance to spread new seeds by sharing your harvest.

GIVING WITH PURPOSE

Even though it is good to spread the wealth, so to speak, you want to be conscious of your giving. There are many ways to give and many reasons to do so. A person may give with expectation or without expectation. The most common philosophy on giving is to do so for the shear joy of it *without* expectation. If you give of yourself, your time or your money and care not if you receive anything in return, that's fantastic, but there is absolutely *nothing* wrong with giving for the purpose of receiving. If we were completely honest with ourselves, we would admit that for the most part, we give with the underlying hope of receiving at least blessings from heaven. Don't feel guilty! At the end of the day, it really doesn't matter what your underlying reasons are for giving, the results are still the same; someone benefits.

Let's say, a business buys a bunch of turkeys and sends them to the Salvation Army for the sole purpose of using the gift as a tax right-off. On Christmas day, 200 homeless souls go to the Salvation Army kitchen for a warm holiday meal. Do you think the 200 individuals care who gave the turkeys? Do you think these 200 individuals gave so much as a single thought as to *why* the donor gave the turkeys? The answers are; NO and NO! The point I'm trying to make is, for the beneficiary of the gift, it just does not matter *why* someone gave, they are just happy *someone* did.

There are a lot of companies that give to a cause solely for the benefit of advertising. This is called, *Cause Marketing*. This has come to be a popular way for companies to introduce themselves or a new product to the market. The company is simply *giving* to *receive* customer loyalty. There are entertainers who give of their time in some instances to promote a new movie or CD. The consumer is usually well aware of the intentions of the giver, but enjoys the benefit nonetheless. It's what you might call, a *win, win* situation.

In the late nineties, my brother and I opened a kiosk in a shopping mall that sold German-roasted nuts. We would roast them in a mixture of sugar, cinnamon and vanilla and the aroma would saturate the better part of the mall. From open 'til close, my brother and I would stand on either side of the kiosk and offer samples of our fresh roasted nuts to shoppers passing by in hopes that they would like the taste and become loyal customers. Of course, there were a lot of nuts handed out on any given day that did not gain immediate business, but we certainly came out ahead.

Now, the potential customer knew our intentions, but enjoyed the free sample nonetheless. My brother and I were basically using the samples as a way of sowing seeds in hopes that they would grow to become satisfied customers. The customers would then spawn other seeds by sharing the nuts they had purchased or tell a friend or family member generating additional business. This is what I call *giving with purpose.*

Now, let's deal with *your* reasons for giving. When it comes to giving *and* receiving, my wife and I have lived by a simple philosophy for the past twenty years that we call *The Universal Account.* It is our belief that we maintain a cosmic bank account that we must keep balanced for as long as we exist in this universe.

For example; if my wife and I were to borrow $500 from a friend, we would subtract the money from our universal account. At this point we know that we have not only accepted help from an individual that most likely expects us to repay the money, but we have in a sense, taken the $500 help from the universe. We would then need to balance our account by repaying the money to the person we borrowed from and then, as soon as the opportunity presented itself, we would either help the same person that helped us or someone else with a need. This would keep our universal account balanced and full in case we would need to make a withdrawal in the future.

It has always been our goal to increase our account balance

as much as we could during the times when we did *not* need help of any kind. We have increased our account in a variety of ways such as, allowing someone to stay in our home when they had no place to go or during transition, tithing, lending a sympathetic ear or shoulder to a friend or family member and of course, lending money within reason, to a friend or family member in a tough spot. My wife and I would view this as *fattening up our account* in case we needed to make a withdrawal in the future.

This does not mean that you give or lend to the point that you hinder your own ability to survive. You will find that some individuals will be more than happy to take full advantage of you once they understand your beliefs in this matter. Do not allow this to happen! You should never give away your entire harvest to anyone unwilling to help themselves. The fact that you give of yourself at all is a blessing and helps your account to grow. We should never allow those around us to take advantage of our good spirit. This would be irresponsible to those that truly depend on you, such as, your children, your spouse and your debtors.

This system has given my wife and I a lot of comfort over the years, but we've had to learn a few lessons along the way. I have experienced individuals who believe that each of us have a responsibility to help other members of our family just because that's what families are for. This is not true! When you see someone close to you continually needing, but never seeming to learn from previous mistakes or trying to better themselves, you do them more harm than good. As long as you just hand over the money, they will always come to you before trying to find a solution on their own.

My wife and I have learned to offer advice first before

money. You can give a man a fish and feed him for a day, or you can teach him to fish and feed him for a lifetime. You do more good giving the person the *ability* to help themselves than you do just giving them a quick-fix. You'll come to know the ones that truly want to be independent. They are the ones that have exhausted every other means before coming to you for help. Be responsible when giving! It's like trying to save a person who is drowning and while flailing about attempting to keep their head above water, they pull you under as well.

Law # 4: *Give as much as you wish to receive.*

PRACTICE GIVING TO RECEIVE

I don't want you to misunderstand my philosophy on giving. There's a big difference between giving with purpose and greed. Greed is all about self. Giving with purpose is a way of sowing seeds of positive expectation. I want you to practice more giving with purpose. Keep in mind that whatever you give you will receive 10-fold. So the next time you tithe at your church, keep in mind that if you give 5 dollars, you will receive 50 dollars in return. If you give mercy to another, you will receive 10 times the mercy in return. If you give of your time, understanding, love or trust, you can expect a return of 10-fold. Giving is a powerful seed and should be done with the expectation of at least 10 times the return.

The next time you're a little low on money, find someone or an organization in need and give an amount that you would like to see 10 times the return. What you are doing is, programming your subconscious mind to increase your investment. Think of this practice as a *universal investment account.* You invest your gift with the intention of receiving a 10-fold return. Try this practice in a variety of ways. If you want more love, then give love. If you would like more respect, then give respect. Make sure that you give exactly what you wish to receive as there is a negative side as well! Understand that if you give hate, you'll receive 10 times the hate.

Would you want to receive 10 times the impatience, distrust, or anger? Again, this goes back to the beginning of the book. Be aware of each seed! Giving with purpose is powerful and should carry positive expectation. There is nothing wrong with giving to receive as long as it is not done out of pure greed. A little later in the book we'll discuss how you can become a *money-magnet*.

BE A GRACIOUS RECEIVER

Never reject another person's gift because you are simply being prideful. If you truly do not want or need the gift, it is okay to politely refuse. If they insist, take it! You can pass it on to someone else who would want or need it if you don't. Other people have a right to invest and grow their universal accounts, so it is your responsibility to allow them to do so. I am a person who truly enjoys giving and would be disappointed if I were not allowed to feel the joy of sharing. Also, I certainly want to fatten-up *my* universal account as well.

If you have a very generous child or spouse, do not interfere with their giving. I've seen this happen many times out of jealousy where someone resents their spouse's generosity, because they feel neglected or cheated. If you have a generous spouse or child, it's a good thing! Be sure to understand that there is a big difference in asking for a gift and simply receiving one offered out of pure joy and generosity. When you *ask* of others, you are making a withdrawal from *your* universal account and must replace what was taken. When you receive what is *offered*, you actually help someone increase their account. You see, there's just as much value in receiving as there is in giving. Make sure to ask yourself, *"Am I taking or receiving?."*

STUDY A MASTER TO BECOME A MASTER
One of the great things about living in today's world of abundance and
opportunity is that almost everything you want to do has already been done by someone else.
Jack Canfield
Coauthor of Chicken Soup for the Soul and
Author of The Success Principles

History is littered with individuals that have in some cases, single-handedly changed the world around them. A master of the seed is one who has become aware of the power of what they sow and has made a decision to influence their circumstances. As I said earlier in the book; *"With great power comes great responsibility."* The challenge here is that the majority of us don't understand the true magnitude of the power we possess as endless bags of seeds. We float through life from circumstance to circumstance just carelessly dropping seeds to fall wherever they may.

A lot of the seeds by chance, land in fertile soil where some allow us to harvest happiness and success and some force us to harvest misery and heartache. A lot of seeds, some of which would bring greatness to our lives, land in poor, stony soil leaving us feeling incomplete and without control. This lack of seed consciousness and self-control, leads us to ask God or the universe; *"why me?"* It doesn't have to be this way. There are those that have dedicated their lives to sowing seeds of purpose.

You may believe that one person just cannot sow enough to make an impact on the world around you.

You may say of others, *"Of course he can accomplish a mighty harvest. He's rich and successful. He has all the breaks I have never been given."*

Wrong! How do you think they've accomplished all their success? Whether we come into this world with everything or nothing, we all begin with one single seed. Pay close attention to the happy, successful people and if you do a little digging, you'll find first of all, that they faced plenty of adversity and that they created all they currently harvest by persistently and consistently sowing seeds of purpose.

A great example of sowing with purpose is the story of Rick Warren. Mr. Warren grew up with dreams of being a pastor like his father. He goes to seminary and starts a church. He began sowing seeds begging and borrowing while preaching in living rooms. He builds the Saddleback Church in Lake Forest California, taking it from nothing in 1980 to a congregation of more than 20,000 members. Then something really extraordinary happens.

In 2002, Mr. Warren published a book that began with the words "It's not about you." The message was simple: by serving others, you serve God. Since its publication, "The Purpose Driven Life" has sold 30 million copies in English, making it by some accounts, the best-selling hardcover ever. It is a phenomenon, a movement. It has given Mr. Warren access to world leaders at Davos, to corporate chiefs and rock stars. It has generated tens of millions of dollars; enough to pay his own salary back to his church, retroactively, for the past 25 years and enough to launch three foundations. "PDL" allows Warren to "reverse tithe"; he gives away 90 percent of what he earns. How's *that* for giving with purpose? Mr. Warren definitely understands the principal of managing his *universal account.*

Another pastor might be content to diversify into "PDL" DVDs and gift books, but Mr. Warren is much more ambitious. If "2.3 billion people in the world claim to be followers of Jesus," then why not take the next step and mobilize those people to do important things, like stop poverty, improve literacy, feed the hungry, and heal the sick? Conventional relief organizations are fine, but why not tap what Mr. Warren calls *"the faith sector,"* the armies of motivated religious volunteers who are sick and tired of polarizing rhetoric and professional crusaders?

Rick Warren is a true master of the seed. He could sit back and enjoy his success. He could enjoy his wealth and continue on with his congregation while living a life of leisure. Instead, he chose to flex his *universal power muscle* and affect the world he lives in. Mr. Warren decided he would not be content to just sit back and feast on the harvest of his labor. He is driven to see his seeds of success grow to spawn essentially millions or even billions of new seeds that will in turn, grow to spawn still more seeds. By sowing with unselfish purpose, Mr. Rick Warren is literally creating what I call *the infinite harvest.*

This type of harvest happens when a person continually sows with one specific outcome or goal in mind. It's like a farmer planting an over-abundance of corn seed to not only ensure a good harvest, but also to grow enough seed corn to continue the circle of life.

FLEXING THE MUSCLE OF UNIVERSAL POWER

Each of us is directly plugged in to a universal source of energy with *unfathomable* power. All you have to do now is to become aware of your access to this power and make use of it. To direct this powerful energy, you and I have been given an endless supply of seeds to sow that we may grow and harvest anything our hearts desire. Becoming aware of this power and the seeds you have to control it, will help you to become a *master of the seed*. Knowledge is power and you now have it. All you have to do is simply flex your muscle of universal power to impose your will. You have an endless list of examples of masters who have learned to channel the power of the universe through the sowing of seeds.

I shared the stories of Pierre Omidyar and Rick Warren, but let's look at some other masters. As I said before, this is my way of getting you as close as I can to those you wish to be like. To become, act as if.

Brad Pitt and Angelina Jolie have spent years in the press being harassed and pursued for any piece of private life the paparazzi could attain. They finally began to understand that they possessed the power to redirect this aggravation to benefit of others. If the paparazzi were going to follow the couple everywhere, Pitt figured they might as well drag them somewhere that desperately needed the world's attention, Africa.

"It's the first time I've actually felt like we have some degree of control over it," says Pitt.

An example of his new strategy unfolded when he and Jolie sold the much coveted first baby photos of their daughter Shiloh Nouvel to People magazine for a reported $4 million and gave all the money to African charities. Pitt knew that eventually, someone would get the photos, so he took control and flexed his universal muscle to his will. In doing so, he has sown seeds in the minds and hearts of people around the globe that have begun to cause a chain reaction of future harvests for the people of Africa.

Brad is also sowing in America, too. A longtime student of architecture and an advocate of *green* design, Pitt saw an opportunity after Hurricane Katrina to help rebuild New Orleans in an innovative way. Joining forces with Global Green USA, an environmental advocacy group, Pitt put up $100,000 to help sponsor an architecture competition that requires contestants to create affordable, multifamily housing for the city that is eco-friendly and community focused. Global Green has already received more than 3,000 submissions. As you can see, Mr. Brad Pitt is another true master of the seed. It all begins with awareness, one seed and a purpose.

Become an apprentice to the masters; they are all around you. I'm going to give honorable mention to some masters you will know and some you may not have heard of, but look around your community and even amongst your own family and friends. There are plenty of masters you may apprentice to.

I could research the masters and probably give tens of thousands of examples to live by, but I'll keep the list of honorable mentions to a reasonable minimum. I suggest that you do your own due-diligence and research these I mention along with others you may find. This will help you to better understand your connection to the power of the universe and it will also help you to understand through example, how to better sow *your* seeds of purpose to harvest the success you seek.

WANTED: SOMEONE TO APPRENTICE A MASTER OF THE SEED

You can ask any successful person on the planet and you will find that they made study of someone who had gone on before them. They may have listened to motivational CDs or read autobiographies of individuals that achieved the type of success they themselves wished to obtain. Either way, most people (myself included), became an apprentice to others we admired.

At this point, I'm going to share examples of people I deem to be masters of the seed. These examples are more of a display of their sowing seeds of giving, but should you dig a little deeper, you will find that they are able to give so generously because they have previously sown the seeds that grew success in other areas of their lives. True masters live to give. Personal monetary gain is never enough. They truly enjoy sharing their abundance with others.

Remember, to become, act as if. These examples are not to overwhelm you or to make you feel as if you have to set the bar. The point here is to show you how powerful the seeds *you* carry are. I would also suggest that you seek out the autobiographies of some of these individuals. This will give you the advantage of avoiding the hurdles they have faced and should give you a better understanding of the strategies that lead to their successes.

Andre Agassi: His K-12 school benefiting at-risk kids boasts small classes and longer school days.

Tyra Banks: Her summer camp has evolved into a grant-making foundation to support low-income girls.

George Clooney: Trekked to Darfur and headlined the bipartisan events in D.C. to raise awareness.

Dolly Parton: Her program *Imagination Library*, gave about 2 million books last year to 215,000 kids under 5 nationwide.

Perry Jansen: This M.D. moved his family to Malawi in 1999, dedicating his life to HIV/AIDS in Africa.

Robert Kapp: D.C. tax attorney forgoes huge bucks to focus almost entirely on pro bono projects.

Anne Peters: Her East L.A. diabetes clinic serves the underserved and is a model of inner-city outreach.

Cameron Sinclair: Architect quit firm to start nonprofit that lends know-how to tsunami and Katrina rebuilding.

Bill and Melinda Gates: Founders of the world's largest philanthropic organization, the Bill and Melinda Gates Foundation focusing on world health, fighting such diseases as malaria, HIV/AIDS, and tuberculosis, improving U.S. libraries and high schools and bridging the technological gap in underdeveloped countries around the world.

Warren Buffett: Worth $44 billion at the age of 75, began giving away 85% of his wealth in July of 2006. Five-sixths of the contribution will go the *Bill and Melinda Gates Foundation* already worth $30 billion.

There are too many masters to name, much less, provide all the details of their contributions to society. Understand, it doesn't have to be all about charitable contributions when it comes to being a master of the seed. It's simply being conscious of yourself as being tapped into the *universal power grid* and consciously focusing this power for the benefit of yourself *and* others by sowing seeds.

Before we move on to the areas of your life that need seeding and teaching you how to do so, I do want to make a special mention of three individuals that have inspired me to consciously sow my seeds through cause marketing, teaching and even the writing of this book. These three people get a special mention, not because they have out-sown everyone else in the world, but because they have unknowingly allowed me to apprentice to their actions and teachings.

When it comes to the sowing of seeds, it's easy to believe that **Montel Williams** truly understands the infinite power within each and every seed. As an actor, author, teacher and activist, Montel takes advantage of every seed at his disposal.

The *Montel Williams MS Foundation* has made available more $1 million dollars in grants to date, to fund awareness and research benefiting the scientific study of multiple sclerosis. Now, after viewing a few of the previous examples, you probably think this is no big deal. First of all, 1 cent is a big deal if it helps anyone, but with Montel, it's more than that; he has a true, sincere commitment to humanity.

Of late, Montel has begun the mission of making sure that those who cannot afford their medications get the help they need. If you tune in to his daily show, you will see what I have seen for years; he absolutely cares and values every seed. Without going into every show, book and contribution, I just want to encourage you to study this master. He is unique in his approach to serving humanity. He is uninhibited and does not need to be recognized. Although, bringing attention to *your* contribution is not necessarily a bad thing. Sometimes it may serve to heighten others' awareness and inspire them to help. Personally, I just appreciate Montel's approach to sowing seeds of purpose. I assure you, there is much to learn about sowing seeds from this master.

As the world's most sought after success expert, **Anthony Robbins** could be considered by anyone to be the godfather of the masters of the seed. He knows *exactly* what he's doing and what he wants.

Mr. Robbins has personally consulted with 3 U.S. presidents, members of 3 royal families, Mother Theresa, Mikhail Gorbachev (former president of the Soviet Union), various U.S. Congressmen, Nelson Mandela, Margaret Thatcher and the British Parliament, to name a few. Author of multiple best-selling books, Robbins is the creator of the number one personal development system of all time—*Personal Power*—which to date, has sold more than 35 million copies worldwide. Toastmasters International recognized him as one of the world's greatest speakers and awarded Anthony the Golden Gavel Award, their most prestigious honor.

Founder of the *Anthony Robbins Foundation,* Robbins feeds more than one million people every year with the *Basket brigade.* He has initiated programs in 2,046 schools, 758 prisons and more than 100,000 health and human service organizations and homeless shelters to assist the homeless, elderly and inner-city youth. More than 3 million people from over 80 countries have attended Anthony's live seminars or speaking engagements; myself included.

As a master of the seed, Anthony Robbins has taught me more than I could possibly share with you in this one book. In fact, it is my attendance at one of his seminars in the mid 1990s that inspired me to become a speaker and life coach. I had made plans after reading his book *Awaken the Giant*

Within and attending one of his seminars, that I would pursue a career in motivational speaking once my career as a singer and songwriter had peaked. There's no way to calculate how much global abundance has been generated as a result of the seeds of this one master.

Oprah Winfrey is one of my favorite masters. I remember the time she announced that she was considering retiring *The Oprah Winfrey Show*. We should all be very grateful she changed her mind. As an actor, author, teacher and philanthropist, she has sown the world over, some of the most recognized and powerful seeds in history.

What began as a campaign to encourage viewers to collect spare change for 150 scholarships given through *The Boys & Girls Clubs of America* and to volunteer time to build 200 homes for the needy with *Habitat for Humanity*, evolved into the charity known today as *Oprah's Angel Network*.

Through Oprah's Angel Network, Oprah has been responsible for building rural schools in 10 different countries (China, Ecuador, Ghana, Guatemala, Haiti, India, Mexico, Nicaragua, Sierra Leone and Tanzania). Thirty-four schools have been built through *Kids Can Free the Children,* providing education for thousands of children in remote areas of the world.

To date, Oprah's Angel Network has raised more than $50 million, including $9 million from viewers responding to the televised coverage of the *Christmas Kindness South Africa 2002* initiative and, as of January 2006, more than $10 million in response to Hurricane Katrina.

In connection to programming on *The Oprah Winfrey Show,* Oprah's Angel Network provides books for under-resourced children in the region where an Oprah's Book Club selection is set. Oprah's Angel Network has distributed Oprah's Book Club

Awards in Beijing, China, St. Petersburg, Russia, Columbia and Mexico.

To make certain her seeds would spawn other seeds, Oprah's Angel Network introduced the *Use Your Life Award* on her show in 2000 and has to date awarded it to individuals who, though their charitable organizations, are making a difference in the lives of others. To date, 54 Use Your Life Awards have been presented, totaling more than $6 million in funding. The Use Your Life Award helps small to medium-sized organizations expand their programs in order to help more people in need.

You can see why Oprah would be one of my favorite masters. A true master of the seed not only understands the power of the seeds they possess, and does so consciously, but they get involved to make sure the harvest is bountiful so that many may benefit.

There are many average, ordinary individuals to take note of as well; teachers, pastors, social service representatives and local activists, to name a few. The point here is that you have no shortage of examples to learn from. You *can* and *will* impact your life and the world around you if you choose to sow your seed consciously.

Through my experiences as a life coach and public speaker, I have found that the journeys and successes of others can act as a powerful motivator. The study of others can be helpful by serving as a basic mark of measurement to help you set your own personal goals.

From this moment on, it's all about *you*. You can't decide what, where, when, why and how to sow, without an understanding of the 3 most powerful seeds in the universe.

Law # 5: *To become a master of the seed one must first become an apprentice.*

III

*THE 3 UNIVERSAL SEEDS
OF POWER*
*Within each of us lies a wellspring of abundance
and the seeds of opportunity.*
Sarah Ban Breathnach
Author of Simple Abundance

From this moment on we will role up our sleeves and work together. We have tilled the universal soil, we have become aware of the unlimited powerful seeds we possess and we have decided what areas of our life-garden we wish to see the most abundant harvest. Now let's get to work!

To harness the infinite power of the universe, you need only to know three seeds and to know them well. The 3 seeds are:

-The seed of thought
-The seed of word
-The seed of action

Each of these seeds comes in a variety. For instance; with the tomato seed you have the Big Boy tomato, the Early Girl tomato, the Beefsteak tomato and so on. The same goes for corn, cucumbers, beans, cabbage, lettuce, roses, apple trees, cherry trees and; I think you get my point.

The variety is something you will apply as you move through your life-garden sowing your future. The important thing to be aware of is that there are 3 *universal seeds of power.* As you will recall from the beginning of the book, you already are and have always been sowing these seeds. To control your world within the imaginary circle you have taken responsibility for, you must now begin to sow these 3 seeds consciously and with purpose. So, from this moment forward, we will become aware of each seed individually to help you better understand how to sow them in the areas of your life-garden that you feel are in need of abundance.

You must know that as with most seeds, you can't just toss them to the soil, walk away and expect them to bring forth a beautiful, luscious harvest. Although, there are some seeds that will require less attention than others, for the most part, you must be prepared to weed, water and feed what you have sown. As with any garden, you will need to know the proper manner in which to care for all that you have planted. For now, let us begin with the foundation of your garden; the seeds.

THE SEED OF THOUGHT
You are today where your thoughts have brought you; you will be tomorrow where your thoughts take you.
James Allen
Author of *As a Man Thinketh*

You are literally what you think. Everything you can ever hope to be and achieve begins as a seed in your conscious and subconscious mind. As you become aware of the power of the seeds you sow, take a quick moment to review even the past year. Are you currently happy with all that you are reaping?

Really take a close look at the different areas of your life such as, your relationship with your spouse, other family members, co-workers and even your children if you have any. Take a moment to review the seeds you've sown in your community, your career and finance. Are there seeds you regret sowing? Are there seeds you feel you *should* have sown?

As we move forward, you will begin to feel a combination of wonder and regret, but I want you to fight the urge to regret any negative seeds you may have sown up to this point. From now on, they will be examples for you to reference when deciding what you want and don't want in your future garden.

We all have a tendency to feel safe within our own minds. We tend to excuse many of the negative or derogatory thoughts, as we deem them harmless so long as they are not put into words or actions. After all, no one knows our private thoughts and therefore, cannot suffer any consequences as a result of them; or can they? The answer is a resounding *yes*! Other people *can* be affected.

Try to imagine your thoughts as a camera. Every time you think a thought, be it positive or negative; about you or someone else, the flash goes off and a picture is taken. This picture is now what you see. Just as if you were shown a picture of someone you had not met in person. However they appeared in that picture would be what you believe them to look like. Upon meeting them in person, you may find the picture to be completely inaccurate.

A good example would be someone with an eating disorder. I've watched several programs over the past few years on bulimia where the person with this debilitating eating disorder would literally look like an animated skeleton. The most powerful contribution to their disorder was what they thought of themselves. This one lady weighed just a little more than 80 pounds at 5 foot 7 inches tall. When looking in the mirror, she described herself as grotesquely fat. She would outwardly admit that she didn't really believe she was fat, but while looking into the mirror, her thoughts projected a false image back at her.

The power of this lady's thought of being fat was so strong that it literally changed her point of view. Her mind was strong enough to play tricks on her eyes. I am happy to inform you that there *is* therapy that has had success in treating individuals with this disorder.

I learned a very valuable lesson in 2000 while negotiating a recording contract. The attorney for the record label just happened to be the nephew of the owner and while the owner and I had not had a chance to meet before my signing the contract, his nephew had taken the liberty of describing each of our personalities to the other. The picture I had in my mind of the owner was that of a man who was short-fused, unyielding and unforgiving. The picture the owner had in his mind of me was that of an artist who was an uncontrollable, uncompromising outlaw singer with little or no respect for authority. The picture we had of each other was completely inaccurate to say the least. We eventually learned the truth.

The challenge with the *seed of thought* is that, if allowed to take root, it becomes just as real as the nose on your face. The owner of the record label and I lost a lot of valuable time overcoming inaccurate views of each other. We entered our working relationship with our guards up. Of course, as time went on, we became friends, but for the most part, the damage had been done.

We all have had instances where we were forewarned about an individual, a restaurant, a movie or a music CD, causing us to sow a negative seed of thought. We may have taken someone else's word that a restaurant had unsavory food or inadequate service and maybe even passed the word along only to find later we were wrong. Just because someone else did not care for the movie doesn't mean *you* won't like it. The movie *Ishtar* with Warren Beatty and Dustin Hoffman was considered by most critics and movie goers to be less than entertaining, but my wife and I have seen it 50 times. We loved it! Even though I wish to avoid mistakes by learning from those who have gone before me, I still try to exercise responsible caution. When someone sows a negative seed of thought in your mind, it is up to you to verify the facts.

> *Your subconscious mind does not argue with you.*
> *It accepts what your conscious mind decrees.*
> Dr. Joseph Murphy
> Author of *The Power of Your Subconscious Mind*

Right now you're probably saying to yourself, *"There's absolutely no way I can possibly control every thought I think!"* I don't expect you to catch *every* out-going negative seed, but I do want you to make a daily effort to think *with purpose*. It's just like any habit, in time it will become second nature to you. It will be like breathing. Right now, your mind swirls with so much *stinkin' thinkin'* that you don't even notice most of it. A lot of your thought pattern or limiting beliefs have been stamped into your psyche from the time you were born.

Habits are easier created than broken. Your negative thoughts about yourself, others and your environment are nothing more than repetitious habit. Let's try something new here. Instead of you trying to break your old habits and changing your limiting beliefs, let's just repetitiously pump in some new habits and some new beliefs so that we may push the old out the other end.

If you had stagnated water in your water hose and you wanted to replace it with fresh water, which would you think would be easier? Would you rather siphon the old out before pumping new in or would you just turn on the faucet and allow the fresh water to fill the hose and push the stagnant water out the other end? We will just fill your mind with so many new and positive habits through repetition that there won't be enough room for the negative. We'll push out the old with the new.

There's a practice I have used with my children for the past 5 years or so, to help them get A's on their tests. It's a practice I call *brain-branding*. You can apply this technique to anything you want to easily reference at a later date, but I'll show you how I apply it with my children to help them ace their spelling tests.

We used to have our children study their list of spelling words and then test them verbally. If they didn't spell all the words right, they would then go review the words for another 30 minutes and we would test them again. This would spend a whole evening going back and forth until I came up with the brain-branding technique. Brain-branding works likes this:

With their list of words and a clean sheet of paper, the children would speak the 1st word out loud, and then they would write the word down on the piece of paper speaking aloud each letter of the word as they wrote. When the word was complete, they would say the word again. They would say and spell each word on the list 3 times before moving on to the next. Let's do the word faith together.

Step 1. Say the word faith.

Step 2. while writing the word, say each letter: f-a-i-t-h

Step 3. Once you're done writing the word, say it again and then move on to the next word and repeat the three steps for that word.

Make sure you do each word 3 times. The reason I call this technique brain-branding is because your brain is literally getting bombarded by the use of all the senses. First, you can see the word as your pen spells each letter, and then you feel your tongue say the word and each letter, while your ears hear you say it. The act of writing, speaking and spelling each word and each letter causes familiarity in the brain and the repetition of spelling each word 3 times brands the details on the brain. Every time this technique is applied by my children before a test, they get an A.

You will be absolutely amazed at how effective this little technique is. You and I are going to use this same technique to help you sow positive seeds of thought. Most all teachers in the self-help industry suggest writing your goals and dreams or keeping some kind of journal. It helps your conscious mind to program your subconscious mind to focus on what *you* want.

Seek not outside yourself, heaven is within.
Mary Lou Cook

All that you are at this moment, wherever you are in life, everything you possess, in fact, your very existence began as a seed of thought. Thoughts lead to a reality; you're proof of that. From this moment on, you must know and understand the power of your thoughts. What you think of yourself and others is *your* reality for as long as you maintain that thought. As the saying goes; whether you think you can or whether you think you can't, you're right.

Be they positive or negative, your thoughts yield a tremendous amount of power. The seed of thought is the first to hit the soil. Your thoughts will determine what you say and what course of action you will take. The seed of thought becomes the foundation in which you will build upon with the seed of word and the seed of action. Remember the story I shared with you of my relationship with the owner of the record label?

The way we thought of each other in the beginning of our relationship determined the course of our words and actions. It's very important that you become aware of what seeds of thought you sow. I will help you develop the habit of catching and withdrawing the negative, self-defeating seed and replacing it with the more positive, uplifting seed.

You do have a choice. It will take some practice, but you *can* control the manner in which you think of yourself, your situations, and circumstances, and how you think of others. In time you will automatically catch yourself before thinking angry, spiteful thoughts about your spouse or co-worker. You will gradually begin to catch yourself before thinking, *"He's lazy and inconsiderate"* or *"she doesn't love me like she used to."* In a short period of time with a little effort, you will become more responsible when it comes to self-defeating thoughts as well. You will automatically catch yourself before thinking *"This won't work"* or *"I can't do this"* or *"My life stinks."*

PRACTICE LOOKING AT YOUR THOUGHTS

*You are a living magnet. What you attract into your life
is in harmony with your dominant thoughts.*
Brian Tracy

During my *Seeds of Purpose* tele-seminars, I encourage my students to create and maintain what I refer to as, a *livin' the life* journal. The purpose of this journal is to establish a habit of spending a minimum of 20 minutes every evening, writing down every thing that happened during the course of the day that made the author happy.

If someone pays you a compliment, no matter how insignificant, write it down. If a co-worker helped you on the job, even if that co-worker was told to do so by the boss, and it made you happy, write it down in your journal. If you did something nice for someone else and it made you feel proud or good about yourself in any way, write it down. If you so much as have a pleasant thought about your spouse or children, write it down. Nothing derogatory is allowed.

The purpose of this nightly exercise is to develop the habit of paying attention and taking notice of what's positive in your life. We have no problem giving notice to the negative. Really take notice of yourself and others near the end of any given day. When asked, *"How was your day at work?"* more than 80% of what we focus on while referencing our day is what we didn't like or what made us unhappy.

Just like the old question; *if a tree falls in the forest and no one is there to hear it, does it make a sound?* The *livin' the life* journal is an exercise designed to put you in the middle of the forest. In other words, by making it a habit of listing only the things that make you smile or make you happy during the course of each day, you in time will begin to appreciate what I have come to realize; there is a whole lot more good going on than bad. After all, if you don't recognize or appreciate the positive in your daily life, then obviously you're going to tend to focus more on the things and people that make you miserable or unhappy. Just like the tree in the forest; if you don't acknowledge the blessings in your life, are you blessed?

For now, let's write in a separate notebook *all* our seeds of thought, so that we can take a good look at them to decide which ones we *want* to sow and which we want to *avoid* sowing. This little exercise will work much the same way as the one with my children's homework where we brand the *keepers* into our subconscious.

The act of writing your thoughts, seeing them and even saying them will serve to make you more aware of them. This will bring them to the forefront of your consciousness so that you may then better control them. Let's get a notebook and make a list.

You will create two categories. To the left of your sheet of paper, write <u>Negative seeds of thought</u> and to the right of your paper, write <u>Positive seeds of thought</u>. This may make you feel a little uncomfortable at first, but it *will* be worth it.

Under the negative seeds of thought, be thorough and honest. Make note of as many negative, self-defeating, judgmental and fearful thoughts as you feel consume your mind on a daily basis and then you will draw a line over to the positive side and while writing along this line the words *replace with*, you will then create the positive seed of thought that will replace the negative seed of thought. I'll give you an example.

NEGATIVE THOUGHTS   POSITIVE THOUGHTS

I hate my job	*(replace with)*	*This job is just a stepping stone to what I really want*
I have a problem	*(replace with)*	*I have a challenge*
Things will never get better	*(replace with)*	*I'm sowing seeds for tomorrow's success*
I failed	*(replace with)*	*I've learned one more way that doesn't work; next*
She's a terrible waitress	*(replace with)*	*She's just having a challenging day*
I'm broke	*(replace with)*	*my universal account is over-flowing with abundance, should I need to make a withdrawal*
Why do bad things always happen to me?	*(replace with)*	*Gold is tempered by fire. My adversity is a blessing.*

You get the idea. Your list needs to be personal. Make sure you replace a negative thought with *exactly* what you want to think. Remember, your thoughts are seeds you are sowing. Be specific as to what you wish to harvest and give as much detail as you deem necessary. Keep a copy of the list in your pocket or purse and refer to it each time you catch yourself sowing negativity.

DON'T FORGET TO FEED AND WATER

If you want your positive thoughts to take root and grow, you will need to feed and water the seeds. The manner in which you feed and water your garden applies to all 3 seeds; the seed of thought, the seed of word and the seed of action.

You must fertilize each seed with *expectation* and water with *faith*. There has never been a time that I have planted a garden that I didn't fully believe *and* expect to harvest. For example, when you refer to your financial situation as you having an over-flowing universal account of abundance, you *must* believe without a doubt that your wants and needs will be met and just as important, you must *expect* it without reservation.

Remember, your subconscious mind does exactly what you tell it to do and the subconscious mind is the supply line from the universe to you. What you sow with absolute faith and expectation, is what your subconscious mind will order from the universe.

PLACE YOUR ORDER WITH THE UNIVERSE

You have always been able to get anything you want or need from the universe. All you have to do is place the order. I have rarely made New Year's resolutions and when I have, I kept it to myself. One year, I told my wife that exactly 1 year from that date, I would be consistently generating a particular amount of money per month. She asked how I planned to accomplish this and I readily admitted that I was not exactly sure, but I had 100% faith that it would happen. I proceeded to sow seeds daily fully expecting the outcome I desired. I had already sown the seed of thought in *my* mind, but by sowing the seed of word, I was in a sense, sowing the seed of thought in my wife's mind. If I move toward my goal with conviction, she too will give energy to my universal order.

I then set out to sow as many seeds of action as I could to ensure the harvest. By sowing these 3 seeds, I was re-enforcing my order with the universe. Would you believe that exactly one year later, I was generating the amount of money per month that I had planned? I placed my order with the universe, sowed the necessary seeds and then watered with faith and fertilized with expectation.

SHARE THE LOAD

It's not always good to share your dreams and goals with those around you. You're better off in most cases of keeping your plans to yourself to avoid negative input from *stinkin' thinkers*. On the other hand, if you have someone close to you that cares about you and truly wants to see you succeed in life, then it would be a good idea to share your intentions. By sharing your dreams and goals, you can intensify the power of faith and expectation. I shared my plans with my wife, because I knew she believed I could achieve my goal and would therefore, increase the level of faith and expectation and this would add to the feeding and watering of my seeds.

ELBERT WEST

THE SEED OF WORD

You have the right to remain silent. What you say can and will be used against you in the universal court of law.

We've all heard the saying *a picture is worth a thousand words,* but I can't imagine a picture more powerful than the words, *"I love you"* or *"I hate you."* You can even try experimenting with this one if you like, but I assure you that no picture will adequately measure up to looking deeply into the eyes of your husband or wife while holding them close and saying, *"I love you."* No picture can possibly measure up to looking a child in the eyes and saying, *"I'm proud of you"* or saying to an employee, *"You're service here is very much appreciated, thank you."* These verbal expressions are far from a thousand words and you can see how potent they are. Just think what these expressions mean to you.

I know I don't have to explain to you how much power lies in the seed of word. We've all experienced the feeling of warmth that comes from words of affection, the feeling of pride and appreciation that comes from our peers' words of faith and encouragement and the feeling of connection and comfort when we hear a particular song that sounds as if the writer knew our every thought. The emotions are equally stirred by words of hatred, malice and judgment.

As the saying goes, *words can cut like a knife,* so it is imperative that we hold tight to every seed of word within us and be absolutely sure that we want that seed to grow before we give it to soil. Let me say again, *"You reap what you sow."* With every seed of word you lay in fertile soil, you not only begin to transform your thoughts into reality, but you are outwardly describing your wants, needs, expectations and intentions to the world and to the universe. You may be able to apologize once a word or phrase has escaped, but you will never be able to take it back and erase it from the memory of those affected.

A man's belly shall be satisfied with the fruit of his mouth; and with the increase of his lips shall he be filled.
Proverbs 18:20
Death and life are in the power of the tongue: and they that love it shall eat the fruit thereof.
Proverbs 18:21

You will work very hard to tame your seeds of thought. Understand that each of us, no matter how experienced we are, still find ourselves in a constant struggle to direct the proper seeds of thought to our universe so that we may harvest what we truly want. Seeds of thought will slip from time to time, but luckily, you can work with the universe in the privacy of your heart and mind to negotiate the path in which they travel. In other words, thoughts are more easily kept away from doing harm to other people.

Words are a little less forgiving. You may say something in the heat of an argument that at the moment may be your honest feelings and though you may apologize later, the other person will never forget those *honest* words spoken in anger or frustration.

Have you ever been around a friend, family member or a co-worker who's separated from their spouse? Maybe you never really liked their spouse, so while they generously share with you all the nasty little details of the break-up and what a no good so-and-so their ex is, you decide to share your *true* feelings about their spouse as well, thinking you're safe. You may even think you're consoling them. Big mistake! A week later, they get back together and everything is as if it had never happened accept, everything *you* said. Ouch! Wouldn't you like to have those seeds back? Your friend, family member or co-worker will never forget how you *really* feel. They may not bring it up to you, but they'll always remember you saying, *"I never really liked her anyway!"*

Your words are very powerful, so guard them well. Think before you speak. Words not only influence thought, but they also inspire action. The seed of word, if sown with purpose, can build bridges to beautiful dreams and bountiful successes or like a nuclear bomb, they can destroy lives and lead to horrific nightmares. You have most likely experienced both at one time or another. I prefer to help you build bridges and create success.

SPEAK OR DON'T SPEAK WITH PURPOSE

Have you ever blurted-out words in anger to someone you cared about and really *didn't* mean what you said? You would've given anything to have those words back. I'm not just referring to words spoken in anger. Maybe you've committed yourself to someone or to a task only to regret speaking too soon. From now on, we are going to practice aiming our words.

A very good friend of mine shared a valuable analogy that I'll pass along to you. While teaching Sunday school children the importance of controlling one's tongue, my friend Laura took a tube of toothpaste and squeezed out all the contents.

She then asked the children to put the toothpaste back into the tube from which it came. Of course, this was virtually impossible to do and the children made a big mess trying.

She then compared the toothpaste to words; *"Once you've spoken, you can't take it back, so speak responsibly or you will have a mess on your hands."*

I love Laura's analogy and have used it in a similar way to express the danger of what I call *the smoking tongue*. Your words are like a bullet leaving the barrel of a gun, they can be inaccurate and cause injury if spoken out of recklessness and anger, deadly if spoken out of ill intent and impossible to recall once the trigger has been pulled. I've always believed that guns don't kill people; people do. It's not easy managing the tongue, but your future success and happiness depends on your efforts to try.

In the late 1990s I found myself in a boardroom with my attorney and me on one side of the table and my music publishers (a husband and wife partnership) and their attorney on the other side of the table. I was being accused of doing something I did not do. The accusation was being made by the wife. She was accusing me of making a comment that I did not make. Her husband was oblivious to the fact that his wife was being untruthful and was taking her side in the matter. It really wasn't personally aimed at me, she was angry with the gentleman producing my music and by finding a reason to expel me from my contract; she would then have her revenge on him.

The irony in this situation was that I just happen to know she had recently been dishonest with her husband. At this moment I had two choices; I could defend myself by divulging incriminating information about this woman, but I knew it would be hurtful and embarrassing to her husband or I could just apologize for the alleged comment and ask forgiveness for something I did not do. I chose the latter.

I remained under contract and would do so for another eighteen months. Meanwhile, within weeks of this meeting, the husband gained knowledge of the deceptive ways of his wife and had come to understand that what I had done saved him hurt and embarrassment at the time. He later called me and expressed his overwhelming gratitude and respect and the two of us became friends.

I could've easily proven my innocence in that meeting, but at what cost? I decided it wasn't worth hurting an innocent person. In the end, had I shared my information, he would've disliked me almost as much as his wife because of the hurt and embarrassment and I would've definitely been expelled from the contract and lost his respect as well as my *self-respect*.

Choose your words carefully. Your entire future rests on every single word you're about to say. Isn't it worth taking a deep breath and a few minutes of thought before you speak? Don't let anyone rush you into sowing the seed of word. You're better-off not speaking at all if it will cause a negative chain reaction.

SAY WHAT YOU MEAN AND MEAN WHAT YOU SAY

Take all the time you feel you need before speaking; especially when it comes to emotions. If you're going to be in a situation that requires a quick response, such as, a debate or negotiation, then prepare beforehand using every possible scenario. Before I go into a meeting I will make a list of all the possible scenarios and then proceed to practice my responses. If I am presented with a question that I am not absolutely prepared to answer, I pause to think or request a moment of thought.

By choosing your words carefully, you will show others that you are willing to be held accountable for what you say. By choosing your words carefully, you are saying to those around you that your words have value and this will in turn gain their trust and respect.

You most likely have heard the phrase, *"say what you mean, and mean what you say."* As I've said, you may be able to apologize for what you've said, but you can't take it back. You won't have to worry about apologizing or taking something you say back so long as you take the time to make sure you are saying *exactly* what you mean.

Make sure you mean what you say when it comes to matters of the heart. If you don't really love someone, then don't say it just because they're saying it. If someone asks a favor of you and you just don't want to do it, then don't commit to them and spend every spare minute trying to come up with an excuse to get out of it. Make your word valuable.

When my wife and I began dating, she was the first to say *"I love you."* It's not that I didn't love her; it's just that I had had an unsuccessful relationship prior to meeting her and really wanted to be absolutely sure that when I said those three words, it would be forever. I'm sure she would've preferred to hear me say those three words when she first said them, but once I did begin expressing my love for her, she has never had to question my sincerity and as far as I know, doesn't to this day. As of the writing of this book, we've been together for almost 20 years and we're still going strong.

You might as well mean what you say, for those around you will assume you do anyway and hold you accountable.

AIM YOUR WORDS CAREFULLY

Treat the seed of word as though it were as deadly as a bullet and as powerful as a magic wand. With just a few words you can cause as much pain and destruction as a nuclear bomb or with just a few words you can move mountains and make dreams come true.

As you develop the ability to aim your words, you will begin to exercise more control over your world and those in it. Words have the power to give you a tremendous influence over others.

Pay attention to your preacher or a politician and you will see examples of individuals who have developed the ability to influence others with their words. They use your ears and minds as a canvass, painting whatever big beautiful picture they want you to see. You too, can develop your vocabulary to wield power over others.

You have to analyze your current vocabulary and decide which habits must be replaced and they are just habits. In this area, you know your habits better than I. I'll get you started with a few examples and you can take it from there. You need to really scrutinize the manner in which you speak. Remember, every word you speak becomes a seed that will eventually yield a harvest.

OUT WITH THE OLD, IN WITH THE NEW

It's not necessarily going to be easy keeping watch over the seed of word for they tend to fly away without you even noticing for the most part. We all have had more than our share of grief, anger and embarrassment due to ourselves and others' speaking without thinking. It's the old *foot-in-the-mouth* situation that tends to happen out of anger, ignorance, inebriation or just plain inattentiveness.

It's going to take some effort, but in the long-run and even in the short-run you'll be glad you made the change. As time goes by, you will become more and more conscious of your seeds and will therefore, be better able to focus your words, phrases, questions and answers to your advantage.

Having spent the past 20 years in the entertainment business, I learned a lot about being conscious of what you say. From the moment I began pursuing a career as a country music singer I had to become more cautious of my language. After all, it would be quite embarrassing to be in a radio interview or on live television and then let a *4-letter word* slip. From spending a lot of time in nightclubs over the years, I had developed quite a potty-mouth. Not as bad as some, but bad enough. It was very common-place for entertainers to replace certain dirty little 4-letter words with words that sounded the same, but were spelled differently.

A good example would be Davis, a singer I worked with quite a bit in the early nineties. Instead of saying f——-, he would say fudge. Instead of damn, he would say dang and so on. A lot of singers did this, but most would resume their bad words in private. Davis was different; he continued to use the replacement words while out of public view.

When I asked why he spoke with his replacement words even in private he simply said, *"If I continue to use my replacement vocabulary when I'm not in public, then I stand a better chance of never messing up in public."*

Davis was wise to continue with the new vocabulary even when alone. He eventually weaned himself off of the replacement words and I never once heard him use foul language. Where repetition had created the bad habit, he used repetition to create the good habit. When you are around someone who uses foul language every other word, what do you think of that person? Doesn't it take them down a notch in the *class* category? It makes me want to take a shower. When I'm conversing with someone who uses excessive foul language, I can sometimes feel as though I've been sprayed by a flock of pigeons.

Foul language attracts negativity and displays a lack of tact and class. You should hold yourself to a higher standard. Don't allow your peers to influence your language.

DEVELOP A MORE POSITIVE VOCABULARY

By changing your description and definition of yourself, others and situations, you will begin to have a more positive outlook as well as, a more positive outcome. I'll suggest some words and phrases you might use in place of your old negative terminology.

Instead of: *"I'm faced with serious **problems**."*

Try saying: *"I'm presented with interesting **challenges**."*

When we think of a problem, we tend to think of something that requires solving and this way of looking at a situation can at times seem urgent and even insurmountable, but when you look at a situation as more of a challenge, you will tend to view it with less urgency as it is more likely to require strategy to overcome. You tend to see more options when dealing with a challenge than when faced with a problem.

Instead of: *"My attempts to sell this product have failed."*

Try saying: *"I now know what won't work to sell this product. I'll approach it differently from this moment on until I find what **does** work."*

Seeing yourself or any attempt at reaching a goal as a failure can leave you feeling defeated and without hope, but viewing a seemingly failed attempt as just a way of eliminating what doesn't work, to find what does, will keep you motivated and moving forward seeking new paths to reach your desired goals.

The words you use to describe yourself, others and any situation, determines the course of action your subconscious mind will take. For instance; if you say, *"This situation is hopeless,"* your subconscious mind begins to agree with you and does not make any attempt to work on a solution.

If, on the other hand you say, *"This situation is challenging. The solution exists; I just haven't discovered it yet,"* then you have told your subconscious mind that there *is* a solution and that you expect it *will* be found.

Remember, when you make hopeless, negative statements about yourself, other people or a situation, you're not only telling your subconscious mind what to believe, but if you're making these statements to other people, then you are telling *them* what to believe.

Instead of saying: *"This job stinks!"*

Try saying: *"This job is just a pit-stop on my way to the one I really want."*

Instead of saying: *"She doesn't like me."*

Try saying: *"She doesn't know me."*

Remember, we attract what we focus on. When you consistently use self-defeating, negative terminology, you are verbally programming your subconscious mind to focus on creating a self-defeating, negative reality. What do you think you will attract when you make the following statements?

"I'm worried I won't get the promotion."
"I'll never get there on time."
"I'm just unlucky."
"We're broke."
"I can't."
"They won't."
"What if I fail?"
"He doesn't know I exist."
"What if she says no?"
"It probably won't work."
"I'm overwhelmed."
"This situation is hopeless."
"Why do bad things always happen to me?"

You are creating your own reality with thoughts or statements such as these. Again; *you reap what you sow.* These are self-defeating, negative statements you might say to yourself or to other people. Just seeing them written before you is enough to drag you down. Expressing these feelings or thoughts out loud on a daily basis is so much more overwhelming. When you speak these words or phrases, your subconscious mind and the universe accept them as *seeds of fact* and work to make them grow. After all, you *are* king of your world and control all within. If you say it is so, then it *will* be so.

For whatever the mind can conceive and believe, the mind can achieve.

Napoleon Hill
Author of *Think and Grow Rich*

You will notice that we are essentially revisiting some of the same territory as we did in the area concerning the seed of thought. The seed of word, just like the seed of thought, is based on a foundation of conviction. If you or someone else believes what you are saying, then it is so. Keep this in mind when making statements such as those previously listed. Make it a conscious effort to speak what you *want* such as:

"This situation is only temporary; I will bounce back better than ever."

"I **will** succeed; it's just a matter of time."

"I know I can."

"This situation did not turn out the way I would have wanted, but what can I learn from my experience?"

Create a habit of looking for the proverbial *silver lining*. Just like the fourth example, when something doesn't go as planned or work the way you would have wanted them to, always ask the question to yourself or the universe: *"What can I learn from my experience or this situation?"*

My grandmother was a very religious woman and when anyone in the family was experiencing hard times or tragedy, she would empathetically state; *"God never gives you more than you can handle."* My grandmother's statement was meant to console whoever was suffering at the time, but she only referred to the bad things that happen. Whether you choose to refer to the universe or God doesn't it make sense that these beliefs also include the good things that might overwhelm you?

You might wonder why you failed to have success with a particular venture at a particular time in your life or why with all your efforts you haven't become as wealthy as you would like. It might just be that you are still in a learning phase and just maybe God or the universe feels that you are not quite ready yet. Maybe all the pieces to the puzzle haven't yet been acquired.

Just look at some of the tragic stories of those that have won huge unexpected lotteries. Some of these individuals have never so much as even entertained the thought of being a millionaire and therefore have not a single clue as to how to handle the money. Just keep carefully sowing exactly what you want and when the time is right, you will have your harvest.

YOUR WORDS ARE A MAGNET

I used to listen to a personality on talk radio whom I enjoyed, but he had a habit of making a statement that really irritated me. When listeners would call in to ask a question pertaining to the day's topic, most of them would begin by asking, *"How are you doing today?"*

The host would always reply, *"Better than I deserve. How are you?"*

Now I know his statement was intended as a show of humility, but nonetheless, it bothered me to hear him make this statement. I don't believe that he sincerely felt he was doing better than he deserved, but nonetheless, he consistently re-enforced this statement. What happens if the universe decides one day that he's right? What if his listeners decide that he's right? What you consistently say with conviction can and does influence not only the universe, but those with whom you speak as well. I suggest you think and speak what you *really* want. Just because you *think* you don't deserve success or *think* you are a failure doesn't mean you have to speak it or even acknowledge it for that matter.

Though the seed of thought and the seed of word are similar in power, there is one very big difference between the two. The seed of thought affects *you* and the manner in which *you* think of and react to those around you. The seed of word not only affects you, but it also affects and influences the thoughts, words and actions of those around you. Make sure that when you sow the seed of word, that you really want the harvest.

The next time you say *"Life's not fair,"* stop for a second and ask yourself, *"Am I sure I believe this statement and do I really want my subconscious mind and the universe to accept this statement as a fact?"*

Try saying, *"Things always seem to work out in my favor. Life sure is a wonderful and exciting journey."* What does it hurt to pump the universe with positive programming? Lie to your subconscious mind until you and it begin to believe what you're saying.

If you say to someone, *"I am a great plumber,"* then they have no choice but to believe you *are* a great plumber until they have either heard differently from someone else or until you prove differently by your own actions. We all have the power of influencing the faith and opinions of others by the words we sow. You must understand that you exercise a great deal of power when speaking of others as well. If you tell a friend not to use a certain babysitter because of a personal experience, then your friend, having faith in you, will most likely take your word for it as they wouldn't want to take unnecessary risks with their child. You have just used your words to influence a particular outcome by sowing a negative seed against the babysitter.

I'm not saying that what you did with the babysitter was wrong. You know your heart in this matter. If the babysitter did a poor job with your children and you feel you were protecting your friend's children in some way, then you did the right thing by speaking out. If you were exercising revenge or were being deceitful in any way to cause unwarranted harm to the babysitter, you know you will eventually reap what you have sown.

WORDS CAN CUT LIKE A KNIFE

Use your words responsibly. Don't gossip or make jokes of others in poor taste. If you are belittling someone in their absence just to entertain yours and their peers, you are sowing the seed of word irresponsibly. Little jokes you think are harmless can cause the other person's peers to think it's ok to treat them with less respect.

I have a friend who is about 5 feet, 7 inches tall. Most would agree his height is at least a couple inches shy of the average American male. My friend and I, along with a few others used to get together every Saturday night for a friendly game of poker. It was customary for the group of us to talk a little trash about each other throughout the poker game, but all in fun.

There was one other individual in our group that was actually an inch shorter, but my friend made an easier target to pick on due to the obvious fact that his size bothered him. The poker-night trash talk was well received by all and would've continued to be light-hearted except for one little challenge; it had become a little one-sided.

Over time it seemed that instead of the harassment being evenly distributed, everyone seemed to focus on my friend; including myself. I began to notice that we were all making fun of his height away from the poker table even in mixed company. It dawned on me one day while a couple of the others were sharing jokes about size using this person as the punchline, that things had gotten out of hand; he wasn't even in the room.

Little by little we had taken an innocent ribbing and turned it into an attack on his dignity. These seemingly harmless jokes about height had become so common-place that it wasn't until this little revelation that I began to exclude myself from the jokes and take notice of the look in my friend's eyes while he attempted to make jokes in self-defense.

The look in his eyes let me know that the jokes weren't funny anymore. We had unwittingly taken away his ability to earn or demand respect from any of us. Words can be very powerful and as I've said several times before; with great power comes great responsibility. Once you've purposely used words to cause harm or hurt to an individual be it directly or indirectly, they can never be taken back.

At this moment, how many instances can you recall where someone has said something hurtful to you? Even though you may have forgiven them, you will *never* forget.

Instead of using the seed of word to grow resentment, anger and distrust from your peers, you should be focusing your words to lift them up. Be conscious of each and every seed of word you sow. When you speak with the purpose of lifting those around you to heights of greatness, they in turn, will lift you up, but when you speak with the purpose of tearing another person down, believe me, the time will come when that person may just fail to hear your plea for help.

If your words are honest, you will attract honesty. If you speak with the conviction of hope and vision, others will follow you and work tirelessly to make *your* dreams reality. You must understand that words inspire action, both yours and others'. It's up to you as to whether those actions will be *for* you or *against* you. Don't participate in petty gossip and don't allow yourself to become a link in the *chain of rumors.*

In other words, if you hear a rumor or some juicy little gossip concerning another person or group of people, don't pass it along to others. It doesn't matter if it's true or not. Even when I know for a fact of a person's short-comings and someone asks my opinion of them, I don't share my opinion unless it serves to protect the person asking. Otherwise, I feel it would be a negative seed sown unnecessarily. It's not my place nor is it yours, to sit in judgment of others and sow seeds that will work against them. Again, *you reap what you sow.*

Don't forget to feed and water! Remember to fertilize your seeds of word with expectation and water them with faith. You have heard the masters preach the use of positive affirmations for years; this is because it works! If you're sowing seeds to harvest financial independence, you may re-enforce your expectation of attaining this goal by affirming to yourself in the present tense; *"I am reaping an abundance of wealth from the many seeds of financial independence I have sown. I wholeheartedly accept this reality for I am worthy."*

When you speak of your success in the present tense, your subconscious mind and the universe believe it to be a reality. So move forward in faith and expectation, but more importantly, act as if it has already happened.

THE SEED OF ACTION
Actions speak louder than words.
Mom

I'm sure the quote above originated from another source, but my mother was the first person to say it to me. If I had said or done something that required my apology, she would say, *"Well that's fine honey, but actions speak louder than words."* I have come to understand the value in her statement.

When I first had the idea for writing this book, I thought about it day and night. I was already teaching the *seeds of purpose* principals in my workshops and seminars and the thought of reaching a larger audience by publishing these principals really excited me, but at that point, the book was nothing more than a thought. I remember when I first told my wife of my idea to write this book. She too was excited and quickly asked, *"When are you going to begin?"* I responded, *"I'll begin once I've put a little more thought into it."*

I thought about the book for more than a year. I talked about my book for more than a year. In fact, I had thought about it and talked about it so much that I could literally quote you every word of this book from cover to cover, but I had yet to type the first word. No action, no book; Get it?

As I said earlier, words can be a powerful tool to inspire action and I received the much needed inspiration to move forward with this book from a most unexpected source. My friend and renowned medium Mary Occhino, author of *Beyond These Four Walls* and *Sign of the Dove* and a regular guest on the *Deepak Chopra* radio show, spoke the inspiration I needed one night while appearing as a guest on one of my life coaching tele-seminars.

Mary was invited to do readings for my audience and while I had not intended to present myself for a reading, I could not resist. The first words Mary said were, *"Elbert, you need to finish the book!"*

Now understand she had no way of knowing about this book as I had not so much as breathed one word about it to her. I responded by saying, *"Mary, I have two books in the works at this time; which one are you referring to?"*

She said, *"Elbert, you know which one I'm talking about. It's the one that will help a lot of people. You know which one I'm referring to."* I was stunned. I awoke the very next morning and began writing the words you are reading now. Thank you Mary!

All the positive thinking and words of positive affirmation won't get you from point A to the point where you want to be. You must take action. Ask anyone who's achieved any form of success you deem impressive and they will tell you that the secret to their success is action. There comes a point when you have to get on with it!

KEEP YOUR EMOTIONS IN CHECK

The spark that ignites the burn to action is *emotion*. Mary's words evoked an emotional response from me. I procrastinated writing this book when it was to satisfy my own personal want or need, but upon hearing Mary express a potential need by others to read this book, I felt an obligation to follow through. Let us take a look at some of the emotions that have compelled you to take action or to *not* take action at various points in your life:

- Anger
- Frustration
- A want or need by you or someone else
- Fear
- Greed
- Unworthiness or the pursuit of self-worth
- Satisfaction or dissatisfaction
- Pain or hurt feelings
- Love
- Hate

There is nothing wrong with emotions inspiring the action, but you *must* be careful; you don't want the emotion *driving* the action. Emotions can be a positive tool that inspire you to act, but don't allow irrational emotions to blur your judgment causing you to harvest dissatisfaction and regret. A good example would be the story of the Warhnol brothers.

James Warhnol and his brother David inherited 42 Acers of land upon their father's death. Both were contractors by trade, so they agreed to split the land with the intention of each building a house for their individual families. The brothers began the construction of their houses at the same time and all was going well until one day jokingly, David wagered that he would complete the building of his house a month before James. Though the brothers had always been competitive, James informed David that this was virtually impossible as he would surely compromise the quality of his house, but David insisted that he would out-perform his brother while maintaining the quality of his work simply because he was a better builder.

The insistence of superiority by David angered James driving him to accept the wager. James was now determined to show his brother who the better builder truly was. James did eventually win the wager and both brothers did manage to complete their houses more quickly than usual, but in the end, they sacrificed quality and both found themselves unsatisfied with the end result. James knew better, but his brother's display of arrogance provoked him to change the purpose of his actions.

It's ok to let your emotions spark the fire; just make sure you sow each seed of action knowing exactly how it will affect your harvest.

You will either be moved to action or hesitate to act depending on the emotion. For instance, you may procrastinate taking action for fear of failure or being ridiculed. You may rush carelessly to action due to anger, frustration or greed. One thing for sure is no matter what emotion you're experiencing at the moment, you will eventually begin sowing seeds of actions. Our goal here is to help you to sow these seeds consciously and with purpose. In other words, no matter what emotions inspire you to a specific action, you do not want these emotions to be the fuel that drives the action. Emotions are too unpredictable and cannot be trusted.

You may have heard or read the phrase, *feel the fear and do it anyway*. Take a good look at the emotions above and from this point forward, ask yourself, *"What emotion or emotions are compelling me to take this action?"* or *"What emotion or emotions are preventing me from taking this action?"*

This will help you to decide the *proper* seed of action to sow. Whether your actions are provoked by negative emotions or positive emotions, you will want to take a moment to step back and really scrutinize the choice of action. Be aware of the potential harvest!

Emotions can and will spark your burn to sow seeds of action, but *desire* and *vision* will be the absolute combination that lead you to many successful harvests.

DESIRE

*The world stands aside to let anyone pass
who knows where he is going*
David Staff Jordan

From the time I was able to talk in complete sentences, I expressed to my mother, my father and anyone who would lend an ear, my intentions of becoming a singing star. My parents never really understood where I developed this dream as there were no professional singers in the family except an uncle that I had no contact with.

At the age of seven, I made my first guitar by tying a piece of string to each end of a stick of wood. If I heard a song once, I could perform it verbatim. I shared my dream for so long that by the time I reached high school no one bothered to ask what my plans were for the future; they had come to expect that I would just go straight to Nashville upon graduation. My desire was undeniable.

I did eventually make the journey to Nashville, but it wasn't right after graduation. By the time I graduated high school my father had become very ill. He was a diabetic with cardiovascular disease, cancer, failing kidneys, emphysema and siroccos of the liver. As if his medical challenges weren't enough, he was also a manic depressive alcoholic. I was very anxious to get to Nashville to get on with my dream, but I felt my father was not long for this world and I wanted to enjoy every minute I could with him, so I stayed close by.

In February of 1987 my father committed suicide. He had been going through a long spell of depression and unlike the times before, this time he didn't snap out of it. Though he had always been my toughest critic, I knew my father was proud of my talent and my conviction. At his funeral, I became overwhelmed with a renewed sense of purpose to make my father proud of me; I was going to make my dream come true to honor his memory.

I was moved to action by the emotion of the moment. Within 30 days of my father's funeral, I was in my old Ford Grenada making the 5 hour journey to Nashville, Tennessee from my family's home in Bristol, Virginia. I cried 3 out of the 5 hour journey to Nashville. It was a very emotional trip. Here's where emotions can leave you cold.

Upon arriving in Nashville, I took a job working for my uncle in a brick yard. As the weeks and months wore on, the emotions of my father's death began to fade and I found myself faced with the question of truth; *is my desire to succeed as a singer and songwriter strong enough to warrant the sacrifices I will need to make?*

You see, emotions will move you to take the action, but without a burning *desire*, you won't have the fuel necessary to go the distance. Emotions can change like the weather, but desire will drive you to make your *vision* a reality.

PAINT THE BIG PICTURE
ONE STROKE AT A TIME

Most people just won't sow so much as the first seed of action without the perfect plan in place and the ability to see absolutely every detail of their *big picture*. I used to be quick to fire-off the quote: *If you can see the obstacles, you've taken your eyes off the goal.*

This statement still holds value, but you will find yourself tripping over a lot of little details and stepping over a lot of great opportunities if your eyes are fixed on a goal too far off into the future. You will find that most all successful people in life concentrate on the attainment of smaller short-term goals that together, will allow them to reach their one desired long-term goal. You can't sow one big seed and expect an abundant harvest; you must sow many of them to ensure abundance.

If you want to get from Florida to New York, you know you will need to travel north, but you must be willing to accept that it may take many steps and a lot of twists and turns along the way to get there.

You will find that you will stumble a lot less if your goals are closer to you. In other words, try setting and working towards more immediate, short-term goals. This way you will feel a sense of accomplishment as you move toward the completion of your big picture, as well as, multiple waves of satisfaction to reward your efforts along the way.

You don't necessarily have to see the entire *big picture* before you take the first step. All you need to know at the start is the biggest part of what you want, so that you will know in what direction you need to take the first step. For instance, you may know that you want to be wealthy and live in a 5000 square foot house and drive a fancy sports car.

Now, at the moment, you may not have decided just how much money you will need to acquire to deem yourself wealthy, you may not know what style of house or what location and you may not have decided what make and model you want the fancy sports car to be, but knowing that you want these things in the general sense is all you need for you to know in what direction to sow the first seed of action.

A farmer will sow many seeds to harvest one big garden, but he will sow them one at a time. A painter combines many strokes to create a masterpiece, but he too, will paint one stroke at a time. You have to be patient and allow your big picture or *vision* to come together like a puzzle. You have to patiently and purposely sow one seed of action at a time giving value to each one by recognizing each small accomplished goal as one short-term success toward the greater whole. This will allow you to experience some satisfaction along the way.

You don't have to wait until the big harvest to appreciate and enjoy what you sow along the way. I don't wait until I can harvest my entire garden before I enjoy the fruits of my labor. If the tomatoes mature before the corn, I'll harvest the fruits. You must understand that in your *life-garden* some of the seeds you sow will mature more quickly than others and if you wait until everything is perfect or until *all* the seeds have matured, you will have allowed some of the fruits of your labor to spoil needlessly.

Most people give up just when they're about to achieve success.

they quit on the one-yard line. They give up at the last minute of the game, one foot from a winning touchdown.
Ross Perot

As we discussed earlier in the book, you have to decide *exactly* what you want. Close your eyes and visualize the entire picture. Close your eyes and see the entire garden with everything you wish to one day harvest. There's a good reason that other masters have taught the principal of visualization over the years; it works!

Each year, I share a vegetable garden with a 70 year old lady-friend of mine. Over the past 4 years she has become physically unable to help with the hoeing, sowing and tilling that is required, so she has found other ways to make a contribution. At the beginning of our garden season, while I'm tilling and sowing the soil, she will sit nearby with a notebook drawing a chart that shows the rows and what we've sown in each one.

At first I thought I was humoring her by letting her feel useful, but I have come to learn that *her* contribution was just as valuable as my labor. While without her partnership I would normally forget what seeds were planted where until all had sufficiently matured, I now, could refer to her little notebook for the when and where everything was planted, the dates our seeds were expected to germinate and when it was time to water and fertilize. It's one thing to know what you want and take action to get it, but she had taught me how to *chart the course*.

Once you know exactly what you want and why, write it

down. Visualize your dreams and goals and then make a list of the seeds of action you will need to sow in order to make your vision a reality. Make sure to provide as much detail as you can. Remember, the universe depends on *you* for a description of the big picture.

The universe creates using your thoughts, words and actions as the building blocks, so be exact when writing down the necessary action steps required to get where you're going. This will help you to create a road-map that you can use as a checklist. You will be able to check-off the list each seed you've sown toward the intended harvest. I encourage you to celebrate each accomplishment while watching all the pieces of the puzzle come together to form the desired big picture.

Being conscious of every seed you sow and seeing in your mind how each one adds another piece to the puzzle of a desired outcome will help you to stay strong and focused on your journey. Just like the quote by Ross Perot, most people become frustrated and give up because they can't see how all the little pieces of success *and* failure fit together to complete the vision.

Too often, we forget to take notice of the yards we have already overcome on our journey toward the goal line. By counting each yard as a success or as a valuable contribution to the attainment of the desired goal, you will have a better idea as to how far you've come and you are less likely to give up out of frustration only to realize later, just how close you were to the big score.

SAVE NOTHING FOR THE SWIM BACK

We are not victims of circumstances; we are not helpless products of our childhood or at the mercy of unseen dark forces. If our life stinks at this moment, it simply means that we could have, or should have made different choices.
Elbert West

For years Joseph enjoyed the produce his neighbors would share from their garden. Each summer, he would watch with great anticipation as they worked tirelessly hoeing, weeding and watering, to bring forth the most magnificent harvest he had ever seen. Joseph especially looked forward to the tomatoes and though his neighbors were quite generous in their giving, they had only so much to go around for they shared with others as well.

One spring Joseph decided that instead of depending on his neighbors to share their harvest, he too would till a garden so that he could have an abundance of the produce he so enjoyed.

Although he had never before grown a garden, Joseph had faith that his harvest would be abundant. His garden would surely flourish for he was a faithful man and would ask for the touch of God's own hand. Joseph gave considerable thought as to where his garden would need to be and what he would want to harvest. Like his neighbors, he too worked tirelessly hoeing, weeding and watering, but he added one more assurance to his future harvest; he prayed every evening over his little garden for God's blessing.

As the summer months came and went Joseph noticed that something was wrong. While his neighbor's garden flourished, his garden was lifeless. Nothing seemed to grow but weeds. When the time came to harvest, Joseph was disappointed for he felt that God had not given the blessings that were prayed for every evening and he could not understand why.

Feeling angry and confused, Joseph began to pray; *"God, I don't understand! Have I done something to anger you? Did you not hear my prayers asking for your blessings on my little garden?"*

Seeing that Joseph was upset, God replied, *"Joseph, I heard your prayers and you have always had my blessing."*

Even more confused, Joseph replied, *"I did everything that my neighbors have done. I planned my garden to perfection, I worked tirelessly hoeing, weeding and watering and yet my garden remains lifeless while my neighbors enjoy an abundant harvest. What have they done to gain your favor that I haven't?"*

God replied, *"My son, your plan WAS perfect and yes, you worked tirelessly in your garden and yes, you had my blessings, but even I can't help you if you don't sow the seeds."*

Just like a lot of us do, Joseph did everything except to sow the seeds of action. Too often we put together the perfect plan for what we want in life. We talk about what we want, we read books about what we want and how to get it and we may even ask for help from God, the universe and everyone in between, but we fail to sow the seeds of action toward the desired outcome.

There comes a time when you just have to jump in the water and swim. The time and the temperature will *never* be perfect. You must commit yourself to the thing that you want and take purposeful action toward that outcome every single day. If you are truly committed, you must swim with the absolute intention of reaching the other shore and *save nothing for the swim back*! This means that no matter what challenges or adversity you face along the way, you must not make the attempt to turn and swim back to the shore from which you came. Keep stroking forward, for most of time you will be closer to the shore for which you aim than the one from which you started.

ACTIONS + PURPOSE + FAITH + EXPECTATION = SUCCESS!

People are defeated in life not because of lack of ability, but for lack of wholeheartedness. They do not wholeheartedly expect to succeed. Results do not yield themselves to the person who refuses to give himself to the desired results.

Norman Vincent Peale
Author of *The Power of Positive Thinking*

From the beginning of this book I've tried to impress upon you the absolute importance of sowing your seeds with *purpose* as opposed to just wondering through life carelessly dropping seeds and then counting on luck. The only luck that exists is the luck *you* make. I've shared with you the 3 universal seeds of power. If you will dedicate yourself to being conscious of your every thought, word and action and if you will begin to respect and understand the power of these seeds, then you will begin to manipulate your future.

Success doesn't just happen to the person who gets a lucky break. Good things don't just happen to good people. When you see others having financial success, good relationships and good health for example, it means at some point in their lives they got off their butts and went out and got it! This is why the seed of action is so important. The seed of action is what helps you to sow the seed of thought and the seed of word further out. The seed of action carries you to the finish line.

From this moment on, take each action with purpose and expectation. Each day you get out of bed remind yourself of your goals. If you've written them down as I have suggested, then read over them several times asking yourself, *what seeds of action will I need to sow today to harvest my goal or goals?* Now, move forward in the expectation that it will come to pass.

I want you to understand that I do realize there are times when your actions need to be for purposes other than the attainment of a specific goal. For example, your actions may be for the purpose of relaxing with the family or for the purpose of enjoying a carefree vacation. Even actions taken to just *be* serve a purpose. The important thing here is that you're aware of the seeds you sow and this should make you more effective in finding balance in your garden.

WATCH OUT FOR THE WEEDS!

The first thing you need to understand about weeds is that they too begin as a seed. The second thing for you to understand is that weeds grow much faster than anything else in your life-garden. If left unattended, the weeds will grow to over-take various areas of your garden; choking the life out of your dreams and goals. The *weed seeds* also come in the form of thought, word and actions. Don't confuse the weed seeds with seeds of purpose. The *weed seeds of thought* will be the hardest ones to detect for it is near impossible to know when another person is thinking ill of you or having negative thoughts in general. **A few examples of weeds of thought would be:**

- *Thoughts of jealousy by you and by others toward you.*
- *Thoughts of hatred by you and by others toward you.*
- *Thoughts of regret by you.*
- *Thoughts of self-doubt.*
- *Thoughts of unworthiness.*

You can see now why these weeds of thought are so hard to manage. The weeds in the thought area of your life-garden are mostly emotional, and whether they derive from you or someone else, they are hard to get out by the root. In some cases you will depend on your seeds to outgrow the weeds brought on by you and others.

I don't want you to get confused in the area of weeds. Weeds are simply the kinds of thoughts, words and actions that can serve no good purpose and spread to choke out *everything* in your garden. For example: You want tomatoes, but you sow the seeds that grow corn. Even though you feel you are stuck with something other than what you truly wanted, you can still eat the corn if you have too. The weeds can't be made to work for *any* good at all and unlike the corn, can't be used as a substitute.

The same principals will apply when it comes to the *weed seed of word* and the *weed seed of action*. Although weeds sown as words and actions will be much easier to detect, you must not take them lightly. Get rid of any and *all* weeds as soon as you find them! A few examples of weeds of word would be:

- *Gossip or rumors by you and others.*
- *Lies told by you of others and by others of you.*
- *Words or statements spoken in anger. Remember, you can apologize, but you can't take them back! These are seeds*

sown that will generate the worst kind of weeds. Angry words will cause resentment that can lead to revenge.
- *Cynicism and negative criticism with ill intent*
- *Cynicism and negative criticism from well-meaning friends and family.*

A few examples of weeds of action would be:
- *Revenge by you against others and by others against you.*
- *Procrastination.*
- *Theft by you of others and theft by others of you. You know what doesn't belong to you. If a cashier gives you more change than you were owed; you are stealing and causing the cashier to pay the price.*

The choice is yours; you can harvest *exactly* what you want, what you *thought* you wanted, but really don't, or you can harvest a life-garden of weeds. Remember, weeds grow much faster than any other seed in your garden, so think long and hard before you sow the seeds of hatred, lies, and revenge for they will surely over-take all that you hold dear.

Law # 6: *Scrutinize each seed before it is sown. Many lives may depend on it!*

IV

FOCUS THE POWER
OF THE SEED

*Destiny is no matter of chance. It is a matter of choice.
It is not a thing to be waited for, it is
a thing to be achieved.*
William Jennings Bryan

The little exercise I shared with you at the beginning of this book was for the purpose of awakening you to *your* world. If you can just imagine for a moment what it would be like to be the absolute ruler of the world with power over all that resides within, then you can see the reality that I am trying to impress upon you. You *are* the ruler of the world that exists within the imaginary circle around you and therefore, have the power to influence any outcome you wish.

Once you accept the fact that *you* are responsible for all that happens in *your* world, you will then be better able to focus the *3 universal seeds of power* in whatever direction you choose. In a moment, I'm going to show you exactly how to aim and fire, hitting the bull's-eye every single time, but before we begin applying the principals of sowing your seeds with purpose, we must go over a few points.

ELBERT WEST

FEEL THE POWER

We discussed flexing your *universal power muscle* earlier in the book, but I feel it's important to better understand our connection and access to the *universal power source*. Over the past three decades, the scientific community has begun to really study and take serious the power of prayer. They have found numerous cases where people with great illnesses have made miraculous recoveries while claiming it was the power of concentrated prayer. Others have given credit to prayer for giving them the power to overcome great physical and mental obstacles and then there are those who absolutely believe that is was the power of prayer that helped them achieve great fame and fortune. The key words here are: _believe_ and _power_.

We've all seen the football player make a touchdown and then kneel in the in-zone to send up a quick, but sincere *thank you*. We've seen the actor or singer accept an award and then give thanks on national television saying, *"If it weren't for God, all this would not be possible."*

Most of us at one time or another have asked God or the universe or a spirit guide for help, guidance and/or strength. For those of us who believe in a supreme-being or a universal order, the ability to ask for and receive assistance from a *higher power* gives us the confidence of being tethered to a source of power greater than our own. When a person truly believes they are plugged into such a supreme power source, they can and *do* accomplish virtually anything.

I remember watching a television special on the pop star *Madonna* where they were showing all the daily behind-the-scenes activities of her multi-city tour. At one point, she had over-extended her vocal chords and was having a little trouble singing, but by the time she went on stage her voice would sound just fine. She attributed this little miracle to her pre-show ritual. Each night before her show, she would form a circle with some of her band and crew members backstage and pray together. She would ask God to bless her performance and her voice.

Now, a lot of people would say that it was all in her head and to a degree they are right. It matters not what your religious or spiritual beliefs are, if you truly believe you are being directly charged by a supernatural source of energy, you can and *will* accomplish most anything. This is what I'm talking about when I encourage you to *focus the power of your seeds*. All the power of the universe resides in your seeds of thought, word and action. You can literally harvest *anything* your heart desires or make *any* dream a reality.

When Norman Vincent Peale wrote: *A peaceful mind generates power*; he was referring to a mind free of life's daily clutter. Often times, we over-stuff our minds with needless worry and pointless fears. We relive the seeds we've previously sown and wonder what seeds should be sown next to take us to our preferred outcome. A peaceful mind is free of all these anchors. It allows unrestricted flow of power from the universe so that you may recharge and better focus your seeds of purpose.

How does one clear-out the clutter and create a peaceful mind? The answer is *trust*! When you can trust that all the power of the universe *is* at your disposal to create whatever outcome your heart desires, it is *then* that you will free yourself of the anchors of worry, fear and regret and allow yourself to receive a more unrestricted flow of universal power. Trust that all is as it should be and that your needs are met. Go to a quiet place and allow the unlimited flow of universal power to recharge your soul, then relax and confidently sow your seeds while expecting an abundant harvest.

THE EXACT FACTOR
Who decides whether you shall be happy or unhappy?
The answer; you do!
Norman Vincent Peale

I've shared with you multiple times the importance of knowing what you want, but before we move into the discussion on how to *get* what you want, you need to understand the *exact factor*.

The *exact factor* deals with the details of what you want. You see, we *always* get what we want. We *always* find what we seek. *Every* door we knock on opens to us. It is up to us to know and ask for what we *really* want, it is our responsibility to know exactly what we're looking for and it is up to each of us to walk through the doors that open.

If you take a moment and really review your life you will see that you have always received what you have asked for. In the past, the challenge has been that you have failed to provide sufficient details when asking. From this moment on, you are going to practice being more aware of the details when you are asking, so that you may begin to get *exactly* what you want.

You might be thinking to yourself right now; *that's bull! I asked God to make me rich and it hasn't happened!*

Ask yourself these questions:
Did I say how rich?
Did I ask to be rich, but really wanted wealth?
Did I give MY definition of rich?

Did I say when or give a timeline?

Too often we ask for a thing only to be disappointed because it wasn't exactly what we wanted. You need to understand that your subconscious mind receives and transmits information in a very literal manner.

When you make a statement such as, *"I'm broke!"* your subconscious mind accepts this as fact and works to make sure you're right. When you make a request such as, *"I want to be rich!"* your subconscious mind, goes to work with the universe to fill the order as quickly as possible. The challenge here is that without the proper details, your subconscious mind has to determine what would constitute being rich *to you*. For instance, if you're generating $30,000 annually and you're barely making ends meet, your subconscious mind might take your request to be rich and assume that if you were generating twice the amount annually, you would obviously be more comfortable and would then consider yourself rich. Without specific directions your subconscious mind will take the quickest and shortest route to satisfy your request.

It is up to *you* to explain in as many details as you can, *exactly what you want*. Most of us have heard the old saying, *be careful what you wish for, you just might get it*. The fact is, you *will* get it!

> *I always wanted to be somebody, but*
> *I should have been more specific.*
> Lily Tomlin
> Actress

Some years ago, I saw a movie on television where an elder couple bought an old lamp from an antique shop and upon rubbing it a genie appeared to grant them 3 wishes. The genie instructed the couple to be specific when making their wishes, as they would be granted literally. Without much thought, the gentleman blurted-out, *"we would like a million dollars!"*

Without hesitation the genie said, *"It is done."*

Now, the couple couldn't wait for their son to come home from the factory so that they could share the wonderful news. Their son was twenty-five years old and having to work in the factory due to a lack of money to enter college, but all that would soon change.

Later that evening the husband and wife began to get concerned. Their son was two hours late coming home from work and this was not like him. Soon, they heard a knock at the door. A policeman and a representative from the union had come to inform them that their son had died after falling into the machinery he was operating and being shredded to pieces. The couple would now receive a sum of *one million dollars* from an insurance policy they had placed some time ago on their son.

Grief-stricken, the couple called on the genie. *"When we wished for the money, we didn't realize it would come at the loss of our son! The money means nothing without him. Can we wish for our son back?"*

"Yes" said the genie. *"But, as I warned you before, you must remember to be exact in your wish."*

The old man thought for a moment and as he wiped the tears from his eyes he wished, *"We want our son back alive as he was just before he died."* The genie said, *"It is done."*

Within seconds of the genie granting their wish they heard a knock at the door. When they opened the door they stood in horror at the sight of their son. When the father wished him back as he was just before he died, he didn't think about his son being shredded in the machine. I'll end it here.

Even though the story is quite gruesome, it serves to make a great point. When you pray or make a request from whatever supreme source you believe in, make sure you take all the time you need to express the details. When I'm coaching someone on how to place an order with God or the universe, I will strongly suggest they grab a pen and paper and write down their request in as much detail as they can imagine and then have them read it aloud.

Really think about what it is you want, and then make your request *in detail*, leaving nothing to chance. This rule doesn't just apply to God or the universe, but in *all* areas of your life. Be *exact* when you are expressing your wants and needs in your relationship with your spouse, with your children, friends and relatives and with your boss and co-workers. You can't expect others to read your mind.

GET TO THE NITTY-GRITTY WHEN IT COMES TO THE ASKING

Most people find themselves confused and frustrated because they don't feel their wants and needs are being met to their satisfaction. At this very moment *you* may be feeling that you're not receiving as much respect, love, trust or money as you want or need from those around you. You may even feel that you have made your wants and needs quite clear; or have you? Be fair to yourself and others and really scrutinize the details. Make certain that you have expressed your wants and needs with as much clarity as possible. There will be those in life that will not comply with your wants and needs, but there will be many more that will. They just need to know *exactly* what you want and need. I want you to keep in mind that you receive as much as you give. This especially applies in the areas concerning love, respect and trust.

Rehearse the details of your request before you place your order with the universe. When I decide to work with a new client the first question I ask is, *"what do you want?"* The response is always the same. They'll spend 10 minutes sharing with me what seems like a Christmas wish-list of what they want and then I'll ask, *"Now, tell me what you **really** want."*

This always brings about a confused look on their face followed by: *"What do you mean? I just told you what I want!"* My first lesson is always how to ask for and get *exactly what you want*. I begin my relationship with new clients by first teaching them how to explain in easy to understand details exactly what they want. Without this very important information I would not have the slightest idea of how to help these individuals.

Be more aware of your wishes, requests and prayers. Instead of saying *I want to be rich*,

Try saying, *I want to have tremendous, generational wealth in every area of my life. I want this amount of money liquid, this amount of financial value in real-estate holdings, a vacation home that is paid for, I want to be debt-free, I want wealth in the form of good health for my family and me, I want wealth in the form of healthy, creative, happy children, I want wealth in the form of a passionate relationship with my wife and I want all this by such and such date and I want to live to enjoy all this wealth for at least another 50 years.* Basically, get to the nitty-gritty.

The above paragraph is a detailed example for the purpose of teaching you to be as descriptive as you can. Affirm what you want with pictures when you can and use a notebook to write exactly what you want in every detail. There's a reason the masters have preached affirmation over the years; it works! You must train your subconscious mind to place your orders in detail.

Too often, people feel guilty when they ask for *exactly* what they want, for they worry that God, the universe or the people they are associated with will accuse them of being greedy. We are raised in a society that teaches us that asking for more than *just what we need* is self-centered and excessive, so we stop short of asking in great detail for fear of being looked upon as a greedy, ungrateful person. There is no glory in settling for just enough to survive.

Think about your children or those you care about. If you have a choice, wouldn't you want them to have *exactly* what they need and want? When you see your children or others you care about settling for less than their full potential, doesn't this disappoint you?

NEVER FEEL GUILTY FOR ASKING FOR WHAT YOU REALLY WANT! If you want a more passionate relationship with your wife you could say, *"Honey, I want a more passionate relationship."*

Or you could say, *"Honey, I want you to kiss me like you did when we first met. I want to look into your eyes and see the spark that says you're glad to see me **every time** you see me. I would love for the two of us to hold hands more and be alone together more. Honey, I would really love to hear what it is that **you** want. Basically honey, I want a more passionate relationship."*

As you can see, there's a big difference in the two ways you approach your wife for the purpose of establishing a more passionate relationship. The first approach expresses what it is you want, and the second approach expresses *exactly* what you want with all the colorful details. When you ask for something and then think you didn't receive what you had asked for, then it's your fault. You didn't ask for *exactly* what you wanted. So, get rid of the guilt and give some details!

We were not created to just settle! I believe our Creator wants us to have the absolute best life possible. Even with my own children, I do everything within my power to give them the absolute best in life I possibly can within reason. I derive great joy in their satisfaction, happiness and security. From now on, practice asking for *exactly* what you want and do so as if you're worth it.

IF YOU DON'T KNOW WHAT YOU WANT OR WHAT YOU'RE WORTH; WHO DOES?

Those who know me would agree that throughout my life I have always gotten what I wanted. Even though I've been blessed with successes that most people would envy, I have still *left money on the table*. Leaving the proverbial *money on the table* comes from under-valuing one's-self. Sure, I wanted to be a successful songwriter and I got it. I wanted to associate with stars and people of great wealth and power and yes, I got it. I wanted to produce records and I did. I wanted to sign a recording contract and do a music video and I eventually saw that dream realized as well.

It never dawned on me that I should have been more specific in my requests. I learned a valuable lesson one night at a social gathering with representatives from my record label. After a few drinks, the attorney for the record label (who also happens to be the owner's nephew) informed me that I had left a lot of money on the table. I asked him the meaning of his remark and he chuckled and said, *"My uncle would've given you far more than you asked for. The boss instructed me to give you anything you ask. You could've gotten 10 times the amount you settled for. Brother, you left a lot of money on the table."*

Looking back on my life, I can now see the incredible wealth of love, happiness and of course, money that I have *left on the table* all because I did not feel I was deserving or worthy. Thanks to the arrogance of the record label's attorney, I learned a lesson I will never forget. From that moment on, I have increased *my* perception of what I'm worth and have learned to project that value on others.

Upon first meeting you, people are not sure of your value, so they must depend on you to let them know what you're worth. I've learned that among the more successful people in this world, you will garner a great deal of respect if you hold your value high.

It's better to *over-value* yourself than to *under-value* yourself. In 1995 my publishing contract had expired, so I began the mission of searching for a new one. I took meetings with more than 20 different publishing houses before I finally settled on the one I would spend the next 2 years with. Later, while working on my first CD, my producer asked me if I happened to remember a particular publisher. I told him I did remember the gentleman and that I had taken a meeting with him while shopping for a writing contract. I also told my producer that I really liked the publisher, but went elsewhere because he didn't call me back. My producer informed me that the guy really liked me too and felt I was worth what I was asking at the time, but they couldn't afford me. My producer laughed and said something that I hope you carry with you always.

He said, *"That's very cool!"* And I said, *"Why do you say that?"*

He then replied, *"It's better to have someone say you were worth what you asked for, but they couldn't afford you, than to have them say you asked for more than you were worth."*

Set your price high and ask with confidence and even when others disagree with your value, they will still respect the fact that you have such a high opinion of your self-worth. Don't be afraid of *blowing the deal*. Most people will believe you and respectfully request a break on your price or they may decide you *are* worth what you're asking, but they can't afford you at the moment. The point is that *you* determine your worth. When asking God or the universe for what you want, make sure to set the bar a little higher than you are willing to settle for. This way you still come away satisfied.

WHY LEARN FROM *YOUR* MISTAKES WHEN YOU CAN LEARN FROM MINE?

*I've already been all the places you're going and have already made the mistakes you have yet to make. If you want to get there faster and with a whole lot less heartache, I've got the cheat-sheet to **your** life.*
Ron Haffkin
Producer of the rock band, "Dr. Hook"

In my younger days I was pretty sure I had most of life figured out. If someone tried to impose their wisdom upon me, I simply asked to be left alone to *learn from my own mistakes*. Boy what an ignorant, immature thing to say. It's even worse when you hear someone in their mid 30's or 40's make such a statement.

The most successful people I've ever known were those smart enough to realize what they *don't know* and then surround themselves with *those who do*. Why go through the misery and heartache of learning from your *own* mistakes, when you can skip to the head of the line in life by seeking the advice of someone who's gone before you.

On the big decisions involving such issues as money, your children and your personal relationships for example, you should *want* to seek out the wisdom of others. There are just some areas of life that you would want to avoid mistakes as much as possible. Swallow your pride and seek-out those who can advise you in a manner to help you avoid the pit-falls. You don't have to use *every* piece of advice you're given and if you decide not to accept someone else's advice, *do so respectfully* and just say *"thank you."* Don't be so quick to throw their advice back in their face. If you're ungracious, you might find that one day you may want their council and they may not be so willing to help.

Since this entire book is about *me* passing down to *you* the lessons I've learned and the wisdom I've gained, I'm going to share one lesson I learned in 1991. This lesson has been what I believe to be the foundation to all my successes up to this point, and then we'll get on with showing you how to sow *your* seeds with purpose.

JIM VAUGHN'S GOLDEN RULE

Once you begin to live a more conscious life, you will notice people involved in your day to day and the priceless nuggets of wisdom they drop for you to pick-up and pass on. There are lots of lessons I've learned over the years and wisdom I've been blessed with that have lead to my many moments of happiness and success, but I'm going to share this one because it will serve you well in absolutely every area of your life-garden. So, before we cultivate *your* garden, here's a little nugget that I hope will bless your life as much as it has mine.

Jim Vaughn was the financial partner in the publishing company that would share in the success of my 1st hit song *"Sticks and Stones"* for Tracy Lawrence. He was a wise old country bumpkin who just so happened to be a wealthy land owner. Jim seemed to get a kick out of my youth and ignorance and found much joy in tutoring me on life. His nickname for me was "Junior" and, though I was young, I figured out quickly the joy he found in teaching me and was therefore, happy to oblige an old man whom I was very fond of.

One day Jim called me and asked if I could ride with him to an auto dealership for the purpose of driving back to his house, one of two new Suburbans he intended to purchase. Though Jim was a very wealthy man, you would not know it to look at his attire. When we arrived at the dealership; I noticed at least two sales-persons that were not busy. On this day, along with his mountain-man beard and thick-lens eye glasses, Jim just happened to be wearing overalls and a ball cap and they obviously felt no need to hurry as he obviously didn't appear to be someone capable of making a noteworthy purchase.

We waited patiently for 20 minutes while at least three salesmen walked by without so much as a glance in our direction. Noticing that no one had yet attended to us, a young man who had been sweeping the floor came over and asked if he could get the two of us anything to drink. We politely declined and the young man went back to his broom and dustpan.

Obviously irritated, Jim said, *"Follow me Junior and pay close attention. I'm going to teach you a lesson that if you will never forget, will carry you to great success in life."*

I followed Jim to the customer service window where he asked to speak to the sales manager. When the manager arrived he said, *"May I help you gentlemen?"*

Jim responded, *"Sir, I have shopped here for going on 10 years and have always been happy with my choice, but I've been standing in your showroom for more than 20 minutes and the only person that has taken the time to even speak to me is the young man sweeping the floor. Now, I understand that I do not present myself as an individual capable of spending much money, but there are at least two sales persons that have not been serving anyone who could've at least taken a moment to say hello."*

The manager apologized, assuring Jim that the lack of attention had nothing to do with his appearance and while turning to call for a salesperson said, *"I'll get someone over here to speak with you right away Mr. Vaughn!"*

Jim replied, *"No thank you, that won't be necessary as I have an idea of my own."* He then turned and motioned for the young man sweeping the floor to come over. When the young man arrived, Jim put his arm around his shoulders and proceeded to teach my life lesson.

He said, *"I came today to purchase two of your latest model Suburbans. I'm still going to do so, but on these conditions: I will pay sticker price for the automobiles and I will pay with cash, but I want this young man here to be awarded the commission from my purchase. Furthermore, I understand there is a rebate of $2500 on* each automobile and I wish for this young man to receive that money as well."

The sales manager politely responded by saying, *"Sir, this young man is not a salesman, he's working his way through college cleaning-up around the dealership. Please understand that our sales people make their living by commission only and although I understand your reasons, it wouldn't necessarily be fair to our sales people if I allow the commission from your purchase to go to him."*

With the conviction of a man determined to teach us all a valuable lesson, Jim replied, *"Sir, your sales people need to value every potential commission no matter how large or small they think it will be. Understand that you have but one other choice in this matter and that would be for me to buy elsewhere."*

Not wanting to lose the sale, the manager reluctantly agreed and realizing that he had just received a very substantial amount of money, the young college student must've thanked Jim a hundred times before we were handed the keys to the new Suburbans. As Jim handed me the keys to the one I was to drive to his house, he smiled and said, *"Junior, the lesson here is; if you will remember to treat every single person as if they were a millionaire regardless of appearance, background or education, you will never have to regret the one that got away."* Amen!

No matter what area of your life-garden you're concerned with, if you treat *everybody* with the same respect, you will harvest abundance. Since that day, I have made it a point to never assume the value or status of another individual. I treat everyone as if they themselves might be a Bill Gates. Whether you're talking with a homeless person on the street or an individual who is an obvious millionaire, treat them both with the utmost respect and kindness and you will never go wrong. Just reference the *golden rule*.

Now that you have been given what I believe to be my most valuable nugget of wisdom, let us focus the power of your seeds to attain the harvest you desire.

Law # 7: *Treat every person you meet as if they were a millionaire.*

V

THE WHEN, WHERE AND HOW TO SOW

Infinite riches are all around you if you will open your mental eyes and behold the treasure house of infinity within you. There is a gold mine within you from which you can extract everything you need to live life gloriously, joyously, and abundantly.
Joseph Murphy

All you need to enjoy abundance in every area of your life is within you. It has *always* been within you. All that I have shared with you up to this point has been for the purpose of making you aware of your existence and to help you understand that you not only affect *your* world with every seed you sow, but you inadvertently affect that of others as well. This is why you must begin to live more consciously and accept responsibility for the seeds you sow.

Every negative thought, word and action is nothing more than *bad habits* established through a pattern of repetition. Just as you have established bad habits through repetition, you can develop *good habits* through positive repetition as well. As I've said before, when you crowd the pipeline with enough positive, the negative will be forced out of the other end.

I have shared with you the knowledge of the power of the seed and I have shared with you the truth of your own inevitable accountability. You now know by example, what it takes to master the seeds within so that you may focus the power of your seed to attain an abundant harvest. From this point forward we will become pro-active in our individual life-gardens. All the knowledge in the world will mean very little without application, so together, we are going to roll up our sleeves and go to work in *your* garden.

Most masters have developed a system to apply their teachings on a daily basis and I am no different. The principals of this book embody the philosophies and ideals of the many masters before me and although our systems for application may differ, our goals are one and the same and that is, to help you grow to be the best *you* and to help the best *you* harvest a life of abundance.

SOWING SEEDS 3 x 7

As you will see, I have developed a unique system for consciously sowing your seeds on a daily basis in whatever areas of your personal and professional life you feel a lack of abundance. Don't worry; there are no long, drawn-out exercises to do. I have found after years of applying *other* personal growth systems, that delayed gratification without at least *some* immediate reward will tend to cause even the most committed individual to grow tired and begin to stray.

You will find the principal of 3 x 7 to be very direct and simple. Success in my life has always come by way of simplicity, so I am simply passing on to you exactly what has worked for not only me, but other successful people as well.

It doesn't have to take years, months or even weeks to enjoy your blessings. I'm going to show you how to harvest abundance within 7 days. In fact, I've decided to sow seeds alongside you for the first 7 days in each of the specific areas of your life-garden. Here's how *sowing seeds 3 x 7* works.

We will sow seeds for six days and then harvest on the seventh. Remember the question; *"If a tree falls in the forest and no one is there to hear it, does it make a sound?,"* well, what good would it do for you to create abundance if you don't stop and harvest? We are going to focus on certain areas of your personal and professional life. I have found these areas to be of the most importance to the majority of individuals I have either worked with or counseled.

You will find me brief and direct while walking you through the application of the 3 x7. I have found that with some systems, the application part of the teaching can sometimes become complicated and non-practical, so you will find that I wish to give you the tools you need with as much ease as possible.

You may choose which day will be day one, but for now, let's just say that Monday will be your 1st day. Throughout the day on Monday you will sow <u>*3 seeds of thought*</u>, <u>*3 seeds of word*</u> and <u>*3 seeds of action*</u> in whatever area or areas of your garden you need abundance. You will repeat this process for each of 6 days and then on the 7th day you will harvest. By this I mean you will actually take notice and appreciate the changes and positive results in whatever area you are working. It's ok if you sow some of the same seeds throughout the 6 days of the week. Remember, if corn is important to you, then you will want to sow more than just one seed of corn.

Instead of instructing you to get a separate notebook to create your *seeds of purpose journal*, I'm going to add the necessary journal pages at the end of each garden segment so that you may reference the advice in this book while you and I sow seeds of success together for the 1st seven days. Here's how your seeds of purpose journal will work.

Each category will have eight pages. The 1st page will be titled:

***EXACTLY* WHAT I WANT!**

On this page you will record *everything* your heart desires. If you're focusing on relationships, then you will list all you wish to attain or accomplish as it pertains to a specific relationship. MAKE SURE YOU ARE *EXACT* IN YOUR DESCRIPTIONS! Be honest and give as much detail as you can.

If you are seeding the *financial freedom* area of your garden for example, you want to explain *exactly how much wealth you wish to accumulate and by what date, exactly when you want certain events to happen, exactly what kind of business, exactly who of importance you wish to do business with, exactly, exactly, exactly!* Get the point?

This page is very important because it acts as the *work-order* for the universe. The universe *will* give you what you want as quickly as possible, but it depends on *you* to give the details.

Let us say you need a better car to help you get back and forth to work. On your *want page* you write, *I would like a car that runs better than the one I currently have so that I can get to work safely.* The car you currently have is 20 years old and in really bad shape with an oil leak, bald tires, busted muffler and a knocking sound in the engine. It wouldn't take much to do better than what you currently have, would you agree? The universe could provide you with a car that's only 12 years old, not *as* much of an oil leak, pretty descent tires, a quiet muffler and an engine that doesn't knock and you would *literally* be considered in better shape than you were before.

When using your *want page* to place an order with the universe for a better car, why not be a little pickier? Admit it; what you *really* want is a brand new candy-apple red, four-wheel drive Ford F150 pick-up truck. If you're going to be given what you ask for, make sure you're asking for *exactly* what you want!

The *want page* will be the 1st page of each segment and will have every single detail of every thing you want in the area of your garden you are focusing on at that moment. This page will serve as a reference to keep you focused and help you make sure every seed of purpose is accounted for.

The next six pages will be for your six days of sowing. You will write down each seed of thought, word and action that you sow for a particular day and make a note of the weeds you recognize or have extracted from your garden.

Here is an example of what the seed pages will look like:

MY RELATIONSHIP WITH MY PARTNER
(SOWING SEEDS OF PASSION: DAY 1)

Date: _____

Seed of Thought I

_____
_____

Seed of Thought II

_____
_____

Seed of Thought III

_____
_____

Seed of Word I

_____
_____

Seed of Word II

_____
_____

Seed of Word III

_____
_____

Seed of Action I

_____
_____

Seed of Action II

_____
_____

Seed of Action III

_____
_____

"I water these seeds with <u>faith</u> and fertilize them with <u>expectation</u>!"
Weeds to Watch!

_____
_____
_____
_____

The eighth page will be your *harvest*. This is where you will actually give notice to the seeds you have sown over the past 6 days and record the positive changes. Write down your progress and count your blessings. You will be able to write a *thank you note* to God, Jesus, the universe, your spirit guide, your guardian angel or whoever you believe your supreme guide to be.

The important thing to understand is that you can have the most beautiful, luscious garden or the most abundantly successful life, but it will mean nothing if you don't harvest. If you don't harvest the fruit, they will surely wither and die on the vine leaving you hungry and unrewarded for all the tilling, weeding and sowing.

As I have said, I'm going to sow seeds with you for your first seven days in the areas of your *life-garden* that I have found to be the basic foundation in most peoples' lives. You may later want to get a notebook and outline other areas of your garden that you would like to seed. You know better than anyone else in this universe what you would like to one day harvest, but for now, let us work together to seed your foundation.

Law # 8: *Be exact when asking for what you want. Give details!*

MARRIAGE

(SOWING SEEDS OF PASSION)
Love is a temporary madness. It erupts like an earthquake and then subsides. And when it subsides you have to make a decision. You have to work out whether your roots have become so entwined together

that it is inconceivable that you should ever part. Because this is what love is. Love is not breathlessness, it is not excitement, and it is not promulgation of promises of eternal passion. That is just being "in love" which any of us can convince ourselves we are. Love itself is what is left over when being in love has burned away, and this is both an art and fortunate accident. Your mother and I had it, we had roots that grew towards each other ungrounded, and when all the pretty blossoms had fallen from our branches we found we were one tree and not two.

Captain Corelli's Mandolin

In this area of the garden we are focusing on *marriage,* but you may have a need of *sowing seeds of passion* in a relationship with a boyfriend or girlfriend or maybe you refer to your significant-other as your life-partner. The important thing here is that you wish to harvest a more passionate relationship and what relationship is more important than the one with the person we intend to share the rest of our life?

For most couples who have been together long enough for the *new* to wear off, it is a common desire to regain the passion that existed when they first fell in love. Now understand, there *is* a difference between loving someone and being *in love*. Being in love, especially early in a relationship, gives you a feeling of invincibility, euphoria and convenient blindness. Convenient blindness usually exists at the beginning of a relationship when the level of passion is so intense that a person acquires the inability to see their partner's faults and imperfections. When a relationship is new, you love everything about them; their look, smell, touch and even the little imperfections that will later drive you insane with aggravation.

In time, the passion will subside in a relationship, the

intimacy can begin to fade a little and before you know it, you can find yourselves less tolerant and increasingly impatient with each other. Passion often gets put on the backburner when careers become important, children come into the picture or when couples get complacent. We are *all* guilty at times of letting the daily grind get in the way of intimacy.

You might say, *"You can't expect anyone to maintain a passionate relationship over the long-haul!"* Wrong!

You *can* keep passion going strong in your relationship if you are willing to put a little effort into it. You see, people expect the passion to die down over time, so they settle for being intimate as often as convenience will allow. This is where the challenges begin.

If you will think back or pay attention in the future, you will notice that when you are lacking intimacy for any length of time, you and your partner tend to be less tolerant and more impatient with each other. This is because, without intimacy, the two of you are nothing more to each other than roommates. You might say, *"what if I have a physical reason that dampens my desire?"*

You need to understand that when I'm referring to intimacy and passion I'm not necessarily talking about sex. Although, if you have no medical reason that inhibits your ability to have sex with your partner I do suggest that you maintain a balance. The bottom line is that you *can* have passion in your relationship without sex. What if I told you that you can have a marriage or a relationship full of *passion*, *intimacy* and *excitement?* All you have to do is sow the seeds. Together we will sow seeds for six days and on the seventh day you *will* harvest passion.

As I've explained before, I have made available 8 journal pages for you to organize and keep a record of the seeds you sow up through the day you harvest; your *want-page*, six pages to record the six days you sow seeds and a page for the seventh day of harvest. For your *want-page* you need to be *exact* in your description of what you want to harvest in your relationship!

Instead of writing: *I want my wife to be intimate more often,*

Try writing: *I want my wife to kiss me more often and more deeply. I want my wife to say **how much** she loves me. I want my wife to tell me that she respects me and appreciates what I do for our family.*

Can you see the difference? Remember, you are putting in an order with the universe or God and you *will* get exactly what you ask for. Understand also, that as you sow the seeds of thought, word and action in the area of your garden that pertains to the relationship with your partner, you will inspire positive reciprocation by creating an environment of attentiveness, generosity and affection.

For 6 days, you will record the seeds you sow. There are 3 <u>***universal seeds of power***</u>. Each of the six days you will sow 3 seeds of thought, 3 seeds of word and 3 seeds of action. Remember, it's ok if you sow some of the same seeds on different days. It's up to you to decide what you need to harvest more of in your garden. Here's an example:

<u>3 Seeds of Thought</u>
- *Take a moment and think about what made you first fall in love with your spouse and then as you are smiling, write down a short sentence that describes that special moment.*
- *Take a moment and think about the quality you most respect in your spouse and write it down.*
- *Think about a moment when your spouse made you feel the most loved and write it down.*

When you consistently think of your spouse in a positive light, you will begin to notice a change in the degree of tolerance and patience on *your* part towards him or her. When this happens, you will also notice your spouse responding in a positive manner towards *you*.

3 Seeds of Word

- *On no special occasion, look deep into his or her eyes and tell your spouse **how** much you love them and why.*
- *Choose one of the most unrecognized, mundane chores your spouse does on a daily basis and sincerely thank them for doing it.*
- *Tell your spouse what quality you most respect in them.*

These words may come as a pleasant surprise and may even be a little awkward at first, but after just a few days, you will begin to hear equally sincere statements from your spouse.

3 Seeds of Action

- *Decide which chore your spouse dreads doing the most and do it for them. No strings attached!*
- *Turn the channel on your television to a program you wouldn't normally watch, but your spouse would, hand them the remote and then take a moment to sit and watch it with them.*
- *Without notice, suggest the two of you go to a restaurant or retail store that **your partner** favors.*
- *Go out and purchase a "thank you" card and express your appreciation for all the things big and small that your partner does for you, your children and **your** friends and family.*

Can you see how reciprocation will become automatic on the part of your spouse?

These are just a few examples. You will no doubt, think of plenty of seeds to sow; just be creative. You know what will make your partner happy. Remember, to get what *you* want, you must first help someone else get what *they* want. After you have sown seeds for the six days, then it is time to harvest. On your harvest page you will write down all the positive changes you see in your relationship. Count your blessings!

At the end of each page for sowing seeds you will notice I have included an affirmation of *faith* and *expectation*. Make this affirmation a daily habit and your seeds will surely grow! I've also included a section for you to make note of the weeds in each area of your garden. Depending on the area of your garden you are focusing on, the weeds can be any number of potential obstructions. Your weeds can be the negative input or advice of friends and relatives, *your own* self-defeating thoughts, words and actions or the purposeful input or interference of those who wish you ill.

Whatever the weeds are, being conscious of their existence will help you to separate yourself from their negative impact on your *life-garden*. Good luck!

EXACTLY WHAT I WANT FROM MY RELATIONSHIP WITH MY SPOUSE/PARTNER

Date: _____

MY RELATIONSHIP WITH MY PARTNER
(SOWING SEEDS OF PASSION: DAY 1)

Date: _____

Seed of Thought I

_____
_____

Seed of Thought II

_____
_____

Seed of Thought III

_____
_____

Seed of Word I

_____
_____

Seed of Word II

_____
_____

Seed of Word III

_____
_____

Seed of Action I

_____
_____

Seed of Action II

_____
_____

Seed of Action III

_____
_____

"I water these seeds with <u>faith</u> and fertilize them with <u>expectation</u>!"
Weeds to Watch!

_____

_____

_____

_____

MY RELATIONSHIP WITH MY PARTNER
(SOWING SEEDS OF PASSION: DAY 2)

Date: _____

Seed of Thought I

_____
_____

Seed of Thought II

_____
_____

Seed of Thought III

_____
_____

Seed of Word I

_____
_____

Seed of Word II

_____
_____

Seed of Word III

_____
_____

Seed of Action I

_____
_____

Seed of Action II

_____
_____

Seed of Action III

_____
_____

"I water these seeds with <u>faith</u> and fertilize them with <u>expectation</u>!"
Weeds to Watch!

_____
_____
_____
_____

MY RELATIONSHIP WITH MY PARTNER
(SOWING SEEDS OF PASSION: DAY 3)

Date: _____

Seed of Thought I

Seed of Thought II

Seed of Thought III

Seed of Word I

Seed of Word II

Seed of Word III

Seed of Action I

Seed of Action II

Seed of Action III

"I water these seeds with <u>faith</u> and fertilize them with <u>expectation</u>!"

Weeds to Watch!

_____
_____
_____
_____

MY RELATIONSHIP WITH MY PARTNER
(SOWING SEEDS OF PASSION: DAY 4)

Date: _____

Seed of <u>Thought</u> I

_____
_____

Seed of <u>Thought</u> II

_____
_____

Seed of <u>Thought</u> III

_____
_____

Seed of <u>Word</u> I

_____
_____

Seed of <u>Word</u> II

_____
_____

Seed of <u>Word</u> III

_____
_____

Seed of <u>Action</u> I

_____
_____

Seed of <u>Action</u> II

_____
_____

Seed of <u>Action</u> III

_____
_____

"I water these seeds with <u>faith</u> and fertilize them with <u>expectation</u>!"
Weeds to Watch!

_____
_____
_____
_____

MY RELATIONSHIP WITH MY PARTNER
(SOWING SEEDS OF PASSION: DAY 5)

Date: _____

Seed of <u>Thought</u> I

_____

Seed of <u>Thought</u> II

_____

Seed of <u>Thought</u> III

_____

Seed of <u>Word</u> I

_____

Seed of <u>Word</u> II

_____

Seed of <u>Word</u> III

_____

Seed of <u>Action</u> I

_____

Seed of <u>Action</u> II

_____

Seed of <u>Action</u> III

_____

"I water these seeds with <u>faith</u> and fertilize them with <u>expectation</u>!"
Weeds to Watch!

_____

_____

_____

_____

MY RELATIONSHIP WITH MY PARTNER
(SOWING SEEDS OF PASSION: DAY 6)

Date: _____

Seed of Thought I

_____
_____

Seed of Thought II

_____
_____

Seed of Thought III

_____
_____

Seed of Word I

_____
_____

Seed of Word II

_____
_____

Seed of Word III

_____
_____

Seed of Action I

_____
_____

Seed of Action II

_____
_____

Seed of Action III

_____
_____

"I water these seeds with <u>faith</u> and fertilize them with <u>expectation</u>!"
Weeds to Watch!

_____
_____
_____
_____

HARVEST OF PASSION: DAY 7
Date: _____

YOUR OTHER RELATIONSHIPS

We have addressed the most important physical and emotional relationship in your life-garden. We must now address the various other relationships that affect your personal growth and success. As far as which of the relationships you choose to concentrate your *seeds of power* on will be up to you.

This area of your garden is where you will deal with your relationship with various friends, family, co-workers and business associates. You have the choice of focusing on one relationship in particular or you may focus on various individuals as a collective. I have left the appropriate line blank for this purpose.

You *know* what is lacking or what needs improvement in these relationships, so all you need to decide now is, *exactly what it is that you want.*

You may be in need of better communication with your boss or co-workers or better communication between you and your friend or family member. You may feel a need to sow seeds of passion, trust, forgiveness or patience with one or more of these individuals. Whatever your need in this area of your garden, you *will* know what you wish to harvest. Good luck!

EXACTLY
WHAT I WANT FROM MY
RELATIONSHIP WITH _____
Date: _____

_____
_____
_____
_____
_____
_____
_____
_____
_____
_____
_____
_____
_____
_____
_____
_____

MY RELATIONSHIP WITH _____
(SOWING SEEDS OF _____: DAY 1)
Date: _____

Seed of <u>Thought</u> I

_____
_____

Seed of <u>Thought</u> II

_____
_____

Seed of <u>Thought</u> III

_____
_____

Seed of <u>Word</u> I

_____
_____

Seed of <u>Word</u> II

_____
_____

Seed of <u>Word</u> III

_____
_____

Seed of <u>Action</u> I

_____
_____

Seed of <u>Action</u> II

_____
_____

Seed of <u>Action</u> III

_____
_____

"I water these seeds with <u>faith</u> and fertilize them with <u>expectation</u>!"
Weeds to Watch!

MY RELATIONSHIP WITH _____
(SOWING SEEDS OF _____: DAY 2)
Date: _____

Seed of <u>Thought</u> I

Seed of <u>Thought</u> II

Seed of <u>Thought</u> III

Seed of <u>Word</u> I

Seed of <u>Word</u> II

Seed of <u>Word</u> III

Seed of <u>Action</u> I

Seed of <u>Action</u> II

Seed of <u>Action</u> III

"I water these seeds with <u>faith</u> and fertilize them with <u>expectation</u>!"
Weeds to Watch!

_____
_____
_____
_____

MY RELATIONSHIP WITH _____
(SOWING SEEDS OF _____: DAY 3)
Date: _____

Seed of <u>Thought</u> I

_____
_____

Seed of <u>Thought</u> II

_____
_____

Seed of <u>Thought</u> III

_____
_____

Seed of <u>Word</u> I

_____
_____

Seed of <u>Word</u> II

_____
_____

Seed of <u>Word</u> III

_____
_____

Seed of <u>Action</u> I

_____
_____

Seed of <u>Action</u> II

_____
_____

Seed of <u>Action</u> III

_____
_____

"I water these seeds with <u>faith</u> and fertilize them with <u>expectation</u>!"
Weeds to Watch!

_____
_____
_____
_____

MY RELATIONSHIP WITH _____
(SOWING SEEDS OF _____: DAY 4)
Date: _____

Seed of <u>Thought</u> I

_____
_____

Seed of <u>Thought</u> II

_____
_____

Seed of <u>Thought</u> III

_____
_____

Seed of <u>Word</u> I

_____
_____

Seed of <u>Word</u> II

_____
_____

Seed of <u>Word</u> III

_____
_____

Seed of <u>Action</u> I

_____
_____

Seed of <u>Action</u> II

_____
_____

Seed of <u>Action</u> III

_____
_____

"I water these seeds with <u>faith</u> and fertilize them with <u>expectation</u>!"
Weeds to Watch!

_____
_____
_____
_____

MY RELATIONSHIP WITH _____
(SOWING SEEDS OF _____: DAY 5)
Date: _____

Seed of <u>Thought</u> I

_____
_____

Seed of <u>Thought</u> II

_____
_____

Seed of <u>Thought</u> III

_____
_____

Seed of <u>Word</u> I

_____
_____

Seed of <u>Word</u> II

_____
_____

Seed of <u>Word</u> III

_____
_____

Seed of <u>Action</u> I

_____
_____

Seed of <u>Action</u> II

_____
_____

Seed of <u>Action</u> III

_____
_____

"I water these seeds with <u>faith</u> and fertilize them with <u>expectation</u>!"
Weeds to Watch!

_____
_____
_____
_____

MY RELATIONSHIP WITH _____
(SOWING SEEDS OF_____: DAY 6)
Date: _____

Seed of <u>Thought</u> I

_____
_____

Seed of <u>Thought</u> II

_____
_____

Seed of <u>Thought</u> III

_____
_____

Seed of <u>Word</u> I

_____
_____

Seed of <u>Word</u> II

_____
_____

Seed of <u>Word</u> III

_____
_____

Seed of <u>Action</u> I

_____
_____

Seed of <u>Action</u> II

_____
_____

Seed of <u>Action</u> III

_____
_____

"I water these seeds with <u>faith</u> and fertilize them with <u>expectation</u>!"
Weeds to Watch!

_____
_____
_____
_____

HARVEST OF   DAY 7
Date: _____

CHILDREN

*Love your neighbor (and Your Children)
as yourself.*
Phil E. Quinn
Author of *The Golden Rule of Parenting*

As I have said before, *children are some of the most fertile soil in the universe.* Whether you have children or not, you will, at some time or another, influence their lives. For those of you who *have* been blessed with the gift of children and yes, they are a gift and a blessing; you have the wonderful opportunity of shaping *your* future and that of society by positively influencing a child.

As an impoverished child, I suffered from a low sense of *self-worth*. When a child lacks the basic necessities, it's near impossible for them to feel they are loved as much, or as important to others as their peers. My siblings (four brothers and one sister) and I spent eleven years in and out of a non-denominational Christian orphanage in Grundy Virginia called *Mountain Mission School*. This was a place where children were taken when their parents could no longer afford to care for them or in some cases, no longer wanted them.

In the case of my siblings and me, my father was an alcoholic gambler and would at times; disappear for as long as two or three months. Due to my father's need to avoid law enforcement, we usually lived isolated in the Appalachian areas of West Virginia and Virginia, and did not have friends, family or neighbors to go to for help.

During my father's extended absences, we would survive by leaning on each other for hope and at one address, gathering unspoiled food from the city landfill to supplement school lunches. When my mother could no longer conjure hope for the next day, she would take us to the orphanage where she knew we would have a warm place to sleep and 3 meals a day. When my father *did* resurface, we would all be reunited once again.

I share this little piece of my childhood for the purpose of helping you to understand that I *do* know quite a bit about a child's struggle with self-worth. The one very important thing my mother did was to instill in my siblings and me, the hope that one day we would rise above our poverty and have the kind of life that at the time, we could only imagine in our most fantastic dreams. She would constantly teach us that the hard times we were experiencing was God's way of preparing us for great things. She would make us to believe that we *were* special.

Throughout my childhood and especially my teenage years there were what I now call, *guardian angels* who took moments of their time to instill in me a great sense of self worth and hope.

One of the most important angels in my life came to me when I was 14 years old. Looking back, I now realize that I was at that critical age where I would decide to either take the chip on my shoulder and build walls or use that same chip to build bridges. My *angel,* Paula Hoskins, would guide me to build bridges.

Paula was a 24 year old social service worker and at the time, probably did not realize the tremendous amount of influence she had over me. She was beautiful, kind, attentive and understanding and it just so happened that I had a major schoolboy crush on her.

At the time, Paula supervised a new social program for kids from low income families called *Rent-a-Youth*. This program would basically rent teens between the ages of 13 and 17 to people in need of inexpensive labor to help with chores around the house. The Rent-a-Youth program was instrumental in keeping under-privileged teens off drugs and helping them to learn the value of a day's pay.

For most under-privileged teens the program also allowed them to put a few dollars in the family household to help with basic necessities. I'm not sure whether Paula ever knew, but if it weren't for the Rent-a-Youth program, there were many days *my* family would not have had the basic necessities.

I grew to love Paula, for she made me feel as if I could accomplish anything. When I was around her I didn't feel poor; I felt like I was just as good as anyone else. By taking just a little extra time to instill a heightened sense of self worth, she gave me the most powerful tool in the universe; *hope*. With hope I believed I could make all my dreams come true and thanks to Paula and all the other angels that crossed my path over the years, I have seen all my dreams become reality.

As an entertainer, speaker and a life coach I have had the pleasure of working with and influencing the self-esteem of many under-privileged children. While working with kids in foster-care programs I have come to the realization that *all* of society's future greatly depends on the seeds sown at home with these children. The fertile soil that is a child will grow negativity *or* positivity much more quickly than any other soil I know.

My wife and I have really become aware of the power of

our influence concerning the seeds we sow with *our* children. Friends, family and even strangers often express amazement at the level of self-confidence and creativity our children exude. On more than one occasion, we have heard, *"Your kids are about the happiest kids I've ever seen."*

There is a good reason our children are so creative, confident and happy; it is because we *purposely* sow the seeds that grow these attributes! As far as I'm concerned, if you have children, this *should* be the most important part of your garden. I could write a million page book of statistics that will show how a parent's inattentiveness in this area not only has a negative effect on the future of the child, but also on society as a whole. Instead of depressing you with statistics and reminding you of what you should've been doing, I'm going to show you how to sow seeds of purpose from this moment on that will grow happy, healthy, successful children.

A few years ago, my wife and I became aware that we were innocently stifling the growth of self-worth in our children. As parents, we were caring for their daily wants and needs, but we were sowing no seeds that would establish a foundation of their personal value.

We began to analyze our approach and decided that with a few simple changes in our communication and the re-organization of our priorities we could boost their self-confidence from good, to *"I can do anything if I put my mind to it!"* A child with a strong sense of self-worth is less likely to buckle under peer pressure, which as we know, can lead to teenage pregnancies and the experimentation of drugs, among other things.

WALK A MILE IN YOUR CHILD'S SHOES

From now on, try to put yourself in your child's shoes once in a while. Try to see them as people too, with a life independent of your own. For instance, *you* get up, and go to a job where you have to get along with your co-workers and answer to a boss.

Your child gets up and goes to school where he or she has to get along with their peers, answer to multiple teachers, a principle, and then, when they get home from school, they answer to *you*.

You have to manage your time, earn the money, pay the bills and care for your family.

Your child has to manage *their* time, keep up with their school books, prepare for tests, worry about grades, maintain adolescent relationships (which are volatile due to hormones and immaturity), do their homework, do their chores, wash behind their ears, brush their teeth, deal with pimples, learn to tie their shoes (depending on how young they are), learn about life and their reason for existing *AND* then, somehow manage to understand and please *you*, the parents.

I don't know about you, but I don't think I would want to be a child again. At least as an adult you and I have the choice of changing our minds or taking a break and having a cocktail once in a while. We should try to be a lot more supportive and understanding, and a lot less judgmental and demanding.

Over a period of time, my wife and I have developed the habit of *purposely* sowing seeds of confidence, understanding, forgiveness, uninhibited creativity and a heightened sense of self-worth in our children. As you read the next paragraph, see if anything sounds familiar.

The *old* us: We wake the kids for school and complain because they're not getting ready quick enough.

"Hurry up! You're going to miss the bus!" We say.

"For the amount of time you were in the bathroom, there's no way you brushed your teeth well enough!" We say as the youngest boy runs to the front door looking for his shoes while trying not to miss the bus.

As they climb onto the bus, one of us yells out, *"Be good at school today and don't forget to turn in your homework!"*

When they come through the door after school the first words they hear are, *"Alright, who has homework?"*

This is just a very small example of what an average day is like in most homes with children. I want you to take a moment at the end of each day and really scrutinize the communication and interaction with your children. I'm not trying to imply that you're a bad parent if you don't dedicate every waking second to pampering your children. I just want you to *give your kids a break*!

It's a lot of work being a kid these days and you need to take into consideration the fact that they don't have as much experience as you and I to reference when dealing with life's little challenges. Now, I want to share with you the changes my wife and I have made with our children before we begin sowing seeds of purpose with *your* children.

The *new* us: We wake the kids for school and the first thing we do is kiss all over their little faces and ask, *"Did you sleep like an angel?"*

Instead of yelling about not brushing well enough and missing the bus, we help them prepare for school and then kneel down to their eye level, give them a kiss and say, *"I love you. Have a good day at school and do your best."*

When they come home from school, the first thing we ask now is, *"How was your day?"*

We make it a point to snuggle them to sleep as often as possible and whether we are talking to them or just listening, we try to make it a point of doing so at their eye level. You will find that your children will be more likely to share their little secrets and feelings when you take the time to get down to their eye level. It gives them a sense of security for they tend to feel they have your undivided attention. Imagine what it must feel like to have to look up every time you communicate with others. The connection is not as personal. This rule applies to everyone, but especially with children; be a good listener!

When sowing seeds that grow happy, healthy, successful children, try to remember to make it all for *their* benefit. In this area, it's easy to forget that *they* are the ones who should benefit first and foremost, from the harvest.

I'll give you some ideas to get you started.

Seeds of Thought:
- *Take a moment before you scold and think; how would I like it if a stranger scolded my child this way?*
- *Think about how happy you were the day they were born.*
- *Think of a time when your child tried so hard to please you or to win your approval*
- *Think for a moment about how proud you really are of your child.*

Seeds of Word:
- *For no reason at all, kneel down to their eye level and tell them how proud you are of them and say "I love you" every chance you get.*

- *Tell them as often as you can how intelligent they are, how special they are or how talented they are.*
- *Sincerely say "thank you" when they have done any thing to help.*

Seeds of Action:
- *Turn the television off, sit them on your lap or next to you on the couch and ask them what they're thinking about.*
- *Call a few family members and make a big deal of even a small accomplishment. Encourage the family members to get on the phone with your child and show their excitement and pride with your child.*
- *Give them something that means a lot to you such as, a piece of jewelry, an old picture or a family heirloom and let them know that it's because they are trustworthy.*
- *Let them help you do an adult chore such as, baking or fixing something around the house.*

In this area of your garden you will find that weeds will come more from your child's own self-doubt, and the negativity of their friends and peers. This can be avoided by simply earning your child's trust so that they will be more open about what's going on when they are not with you. If they are more willing to share with you what's happening in their little world, then you have a chance to sow the seeds that can help them.

Though my approach to this area of your garden is focused more on younger children, I want you to understand that your child can never be too old to benefit from these principals. Even as adults we may feel the need to gain mom and dad's approval, love and respect. Every adult is *still* someone's child.

*Train up a child in the way he should go; and
When he is old, he will not depart from it*
Proverbs 22:6

EXACTLY WHAT I WANT FOR MY CHILD

Date: _____

_____
_____
_____
_____
_____
_____
_____
_____
_____
_____
_____
_____
_____
_____
_____
_____

MY CHILD
(SOWING SEEDS OF SELF-WORTH: DAY 1)

Date: _____

Seed of <u>Thought</u> I

_____
_____

Seed of <u>Thought</u> II

_____
_____

Seed of <u>Thought</u> III

_____
_____

Seed of <u>Word</u> I

_____
_____

Seed of <u>Word</u> II

_____
_____

Seed of <u>Word</u> III

_____
_____

Seed of <u>Action</u> I

_____
_____

Seed of <u>Action</u> II

_____
_____

Seed of <u>Action</u> III

_____
_____

"I water these seeds with faith and fertilize them with expectation!"
Weeds to Watch!

_____
_____
_____
_____

MY CHILD
(SOWING SEEDS OF SELF-WORTH: DAY 2)

Date: _____

Seed of <u>Thought</u> I

_____
_____

Seed of <u>Thought</u> II

_____
_____

Seed of <u>Thought</u> III

_____
_____

Seed of <u>Word</u> I

_____
_____

Seed of <u>Word</u> II

_____
_____

Seed of <u>Word</u> III

_____
_____

Seed of <u>Action</u> I

_____
_____

Seed of <u>Action</u> II

_____
_____

Seed of <u>Action</u> III

_____
_____

"I water these seeds with <u>faith</u> and fertilize them with <u>expectation</u>!"
Weeds to Watch!

_____
_____
_____
_____

MY CHILD
(SOWING SEEDS OF SELF-WORTH: DAY 3)
Date: _____

Seed of <u>Thought</u> I

Seed of <u>Thought</u> II

Seed of <u>Thought</u> III

Seed of <u>Word</u> I

Seed of <u>Word</u> II

Seed of <u>Word</u> III

Seed of <u>Action</u> I

Seed of <u>Action</u> II

Seed of <u>Action</u> III

"I water these seeds with <u>faith</u> and fertilize them with <u>expectation</u>!"
Weeds to Watch!

_____
_____
_____
_____

MY CHILD
(SOWING SEEDS OF SELF-WORTH: DAY 4)

Date: _____

Seed of <u>Thought</u> I

_____
_____

Seed of <u>Thought</u> II

_____
_____

Seed of <u>Thought</u> III

_____
_____

Seed of <u>Word</u> I

_____
_____

Seed of <u>Word</u> II

_____
_____

Seed of <u>Word</u> III

_____
_____

Seed of <u>Action</u> I

_____
_____

Seed of <u>Action</u> II

_____
_____

Seed of <u>Action</u> III

_____
_____

"I water these seeds with <u>faith</u> and fertilize them with <u>expectation</u>!"
Weeds to Watch!

_____
_____
_____
_____

MY CHILD
(SOWING SEEDS OF SELF-WORTH: DAY 5)
Date: _____

Seed of <u>Thought</u> I

_____
_____

Seed of <u>Thought</u> II

_____
_____

Seed of <u>Thought</u> III

_____
_____

Seed of <u>Word</u> I

_____
_____

Seed of <u>Word</u> II

_____
_____

Seed of <u>Word</u> III

_____
_____

Seed of <u>Action</u> I

_____
_____

Seed of <u>Action</u> II

_____
_____

Seed of <u>Action</u> III

_____
_____

"I water these seeds with <u>faith</u> and fertilize them with <u>expectation</u>!"
Weeds to Watch!

_____
_____
_____
_____

MY CHILD
(SOWING SEEDS OF SELF-WORTH: DAY 6)
Date: _____

Seed of Thought I

_____
_____

Seed of Thought II

_____
_____

Seed of Thought III

_____
_____

Seed of Word I

_____
_____

Seed of Word II

_____
_____

Seed of Word III

_____
_____

Seed of Action I

_____
_____

Seed of Action II

_____
_____

Seed of Action III

_____
_____

"I water these seeds with faith and fertilize them with expectation!"
Weeds to Watch!

_____
_____
_____
_____

HARVEST: DAY 7
Date: _____

HEALTH

Mind, Body and Spirit
When we truly care for ourselves, it becomes possible
to care far more profoundly about other people. The
more alert and sensitive we are to our own needs,
the more loving and generous we can be toward others.
Eda LeShan

Your health is the *most valuable* asset you have in life. Once it is gone, all the money in the world will not replace it. It is irreplaceable! When I refer to health, I don't mean *just* your physical well-being, I'm also referring to your mental and spiritual health as well. It's hard to maintain a productive focus if you don't put a level of importance on nurturing your *mind, body AND spirit*.

If this area of your garden is well cared for, you will find yourself better able to maintain the other areas of your life-garden. You already know whether you need to lose weight or if you need a mental break; the most important contribution here will be commitment on your part.

To nurture ourselves requires more of a commitment and discipline than we are usually willing to give, so you have to decide how important it is to you. I've included this segment in hopes of you understanding that without the health of your mind, body and spirit, you may sacrifice the ability to enjoy your relationships, children and yes, *even your financial freedom.*

You and I are lucky that we live in a more health conscious world these days. There is no shortage of up-to-date knowledge on the latest diet, health supplement or medical breakthroughs. Sowing seeds in this area will determine what your *very* personal needs are. You may need to overcome an addiction or lose some weight. You may need to pray or meditate more. You may need to exercise more. Just remember that success in this area does not come with one seed. You may need to make several attempts to quit smoking for instance, but each attempt must be counted as a seed sown.

I'll make a few suggestions, but *you* will better know your needs and goals. I'm going to mix-up my suggestions to give examples for the mind, body *and* spirit. You have the choice of creating a journal of your own if you need more room here. Remember, I'm only including these journal pages so that we may sow together to establish a foundation for your life-garden.

Seeds of Thought:
- *Find a quiet place and meditate. Develop a mental picture of the YOU **now** to your right and the YOU **that you want to be** to your left and then chose the one you will be from now on.*
- *As many times a day as you can, think of the times when you were at your optimum weight. Go ahead and put an old picture on or in the refrigerator as a symbol of the finish line.*
- *As many times a day as you can or need to, pray to God or talk to your spirit guide or talk to your guardian angel. Don't talk out loud! You need to develop the ability of talking in your mind so that you can have assistance, even in a crowd.*

Seeds of Word:
- *If you are going to lose a certain amount of weight, tell the*

one person who truly cares for you. Tell them your goal, but tell no one else. Then, keep your word.

- *Use a mirror to talk to your body, mind and spirit. Tell them what you want from them. Tell them how they can help each other. You CAN inspire them to work as a team. For instance; tell your body it needs to lose 10 pounds for its own benefit and then tell your mind to support the effort by thinking only of healthy ways to accomplish the desired goal.*
- *When talking to others, speak of your weight-loss as if it has happened. "I have lost 10 pounds!" or "I am successful."*

Seeds of Action:

- *Briskly walk for 45 minutes a day, 4 days a week. A treadmill won't do! You will find a tremendous benefit to the mind, body and spirit.*
- *Go out and buy a copy of the book,* **Prescription for Nutritional Healing***, by authors James F. Balch and Phyllis A. Balch. This book is a practical A-Z reference to Drug-free Remedies using Vitamins, minerals, herbs and food supplements. It also lists many common conditions and illnesses and what the symptoms are. Read this book and others like it even when you don't have an illness or condition. Educate yourself on your body's nutritional choices.*
- *Go to different places of worship. This will help you to understand other religious points of view. There is much to learn from the variety of teachings and believe me; it will do your soul good. Don't be narrow- minded in this area! If you are reading this book and truly believe that YOUR religious congregation is the only one in God's favor, then I suggest you really make it a point of understanding other*

> *points of view. You have a chance for tremendous growth of the spirit here.*
- *Here's a no-brainer; EAT HEALTHY!*
- *You attract what you seek! Seek-out and read the kind of material that will feed your mind and spirit universal wisdom. Read, Read, Read!*

There are a million suggestions in this area, but you have to satisfy yourself. You know what you lack and exactly what you want. The tough part here will be *personal commitment.* The weeds will be your weakness and others' temptations. Watch out!

EXACTLY
WHAT I WANT
MIND, BODY AND SPIRIT
Date: _____

MY HEALTH
(MIND, BODY AND SPIRIT: DAY 1)
Date: _____

Seed of Thought I

_____
_____

Seed of Thought II

_____
_____

Seed of Thought III

_____
_____

Seed of Word I

_____
_____

Seed of Word II

_____
_____

Seed of Word III

_____
_____

Seed of Action I

_____
_____

Seed of Action II

_____
_____

Seed of Action III

_____
_____

"I water these seeds with <u>faith</u> and fertilize them with <u>expectation</u>!"
Weeds to Watch!

_____
_____
_____
_____

MY HEALTH
(MIND, BODY AND SPIRIT: DAY 2)
Date: _____

Seed of Thought I

_____
_____

Seed of Thought II

_____
_____

Seed of Thought III

_____
_____

Seed of Word I

_____
_____

Seed of Word II

_____
_____

Seed of Word III

_____
_____

Seed of Action I

_____
_____

Seed of Action II

_____
_____

Seed of Action III

_____
_____

"I water these seeds with <u>faith</u> and fertilize them with <u>expectation</u>!"
Weeds to Watch!

_____
_____
_____
_____

MY HEALTH
(MIND, BODY AND SPIRIT: DAY 3)
Date: _____

Seed of Thought I

_____
_____

Seed of Thought II

_____
_____

Seed of Thought III

_____
_____

Seed of Word I

_____
_____

Seed of Word II

_____
_____

Seed of Word III

_____
_____

Seed of Action I

_____
_____

Seed of Action II

_____
_____

Seed of Action III

_____
_____

"I water these seeds with <u>faith</u> and fertilize them with <u>expectation</u>!"
Weeds to Watch!

_____
_____
_____
_____

MY HEALTH
(MIND, BODY AND SPIRIT: DAY 4)
Date: _____

Seed of <u>Thought</u> I

_____
_____

Seed of <u>Thought</u> II

_____
_____

Seed of <u>Thought</u> III

_____
_____

Seed of <u>Word</u> I

_____
_____

Seed of <u>Word</u> II

_____
_____

Seed of <u>Word</u> III

_____
_____

Seed of <u>Action</u> I

_____
_____

Seed of <u>Action</u> II

_____
_____

Seed of <u>Action</u> III

_____
_____

"I water these seeds with <u>faith</u> and fertilize them with <u>expectation</u>!"
Weeds to Watch!

_____
_____
_____
_____

MY HEALTH
(MIND, BODY AND SPIRIT: DAY 5)
Date: _____

Seed of <u>Thought</u> I

_____
_____

Seed of <u>Thought</u> II

_____
_____

Seed of <u>Thought</u> III

_____
_____

Seed of <u>Word</u> I

_____
_____

Seed of <u>Word</u> II

_____
_____

Seed of <u>Word</u> III

_____
_____

Seed of <u>Action</u> I

_____
_____

Seed of <u>Action</u> II

_____
_____

Seed of <u>Action</u> III

_____
_____

"I water these seeds with <u>faith</u> and fertilize them with <u>expectation</u>!"
Weeds to Watch!

_____
_____
_____
_____

MY HEALTH
(MIND, BODY AND SPIRIT: DAY 6)
Date: _____

Seed of <u>Thought</u> I

Seed of <u>Thought</u> II

Seed of <u>Thought</u> III

Seed of <u>Word</u> I

Seed of <u>Word</u> II

Seed of <u>Word</u> III

Seed of <u>Action</u> I

Seed of <u>Action</u> II

Seed of <u>Action</u> III

---

*"I water these seeds with <u>*faith*</u> and fertilize them with <u>*expectation*</u>!"*
Weeds to Watch!

_____
_____
_____
_____

HARVEST: DAY 7
Date: _____

WEALTH

A person may be said to be successful when he has mastered the purpose of life, fulfilled himself, found identity, achieved self-respect, served his dependents and friends well, supported good causes, developed the ability to keep his commitments, performed socially useful tasks, and discovered the will of God for his brief stay on earth.
William Stuart McBirnie

Money won't buy happiness, but it *can* afford you the freedom to enjoy the people, things and places that make you happy. I encourage you to seek *wealth* instead of just money. Your ultimate desire should be to be blessed with wealth in *all* areas of your life. A wealth of wonderful relationships, a wealth of good health, a wealth of successful, happy, healthy children and *yes*, a wealth of financial freedom.

I have encountered quite a few financially wealthy individuals who are miserably unhappy. They succeeded in accumulating monetary wealth only to find that they failed to accumulate the wealth that money *can't* buy. Understand, there is nothing wrong with wanting to be filthy rich! I just want you to be sure to describe in absolute detail, what you *really* want when you get to your want-page. Remember, this is your work-order to the universe and it *will* be filled!

I want you to go back and reference the *giving* segment of this book. I have found that when I give regularly or share what I have, no matter how small, I tend to experience an increase in money and opportunities. I can't explain this phenomenon other than to say that *whatever you give, you will receive ten-fold.*

You have heard this statement probably a million times, *"Do the thing that you love and the money will follow"*. This is true because when you are doing what you love, you are using the gifts and talents you were blessed with in this life. When you read the biographies of financially successful people you will find that in most cases they committed their lives to what they truly enjoyed. In fact, in a lot of cases, they did it for free and the money was just gravy on the biscuit, so-to-speak.

As part of your sowing seeds of action, I'm going to suggest that you read the success stories and biographies of those who have risen above the average, such as, *Anthony Robbins, Donald Trump, Robert Kiyosaki, Ricardo R. Bellino, Ray Kroc, Sam Walton, Zig Zigglar, Walt Disney, Thomas Edison,* etc…... There are way too many to list, but masters such as these will inspire and teach you how to walk the path to success.

What we want to work on in this section of your garden is the attainment of wealth in *all* areas of your life. I want you to accumulate *balanced wealth*. Don't worry, we are definitely going to help you sow the seeds of financial freedom. I understand that you wish to be financially independent.

To attract a thing that you want, you have to develop a healthy obsession. You have to become a magnet. If you want a particular woman to date you, then you must become a magnet in order to attract her. In other words, you must sow the seeds that will lead you to a particular harvest. The same thing goes for money. This book uses the principal of consciously sowing seeds for the attainment of a desired outcome or harvest. If you want money, then you must become a *money magnet*. It *is* possible to do this in a healthy positive manner. You don't have to sacrifice other goals or the people you love to attain financial wealth.

If you have seen the movie *It's a Wonderful Life,* you might remember the part where Jimmy Stuart owns a savings and loan during the onset of the Great Depression. At one point, the town's people had become fearful and wanted to withdraw their accounts. After everyone had taken what they wanted from their accounts, there were 2 one dollar bills left. Stuart took the two bills and put them on a tray and implied that maybe the bills will breed and multiply. This is how I want you to think. You want to attract money and multiply.

A SMALLER PERCENTAGE OF SOMETHING IS BETTER THAN 100% OF NOTHING

Let us revisit tithing by way of a unique exercise. I want you to take on an invisible partner. Who your partner will be, will depend upon your spiritual beliefs. Your partner can be God, the universe or your guardian angel, just so long as you understand that your invisible partner will be the supplier of abundance. From this moment forward, you will give the standard 10 % of all you attract to what ever cause you believe your *partner* would want you too. If your partner is God, then you're pretty safe in giving to your church or any cause that blesses those less fortunate. Give with the understanding that what you are doing is upholding your end of the agreement with your invisible partner. This will help you to develop an expectation of a return on your investment.

When you consider the fact that your partner is only receiving 10 % of the wealth, you're making a killing! Keep

SOWING SEEDS OF PURPOSE (HOW TO HARVEST A LIFE ABUNDANT)

track of your true 10 % and keep a log of what you have given. Write a *letter of intent* stating that you will give 10 % of all you receive in money, gifts, etc…to your partner for a return of no less than ten-fold. Do not falter! You don't want to pay interest in this area. Give what belongs to your partner and you will never be alone in your pursuit of wealth.

Speaking of partners, you must understand and accept the fact that no one succeeds without help along the way. You must be willing to share a piece of the pie to become successful at accumulating wealth. A wise individual understands that they will get much further by having access to the resources of others. If you are greedy when you are broke, then others will be less likely to use *their* resources to help *you* become wealthy. If you're willing to share the jackpot, then others will help you get to it.

Here's the story of *"Jackpot Jimmy"*.

While in Las Vegas, Jimmy had been dropping quarters into this one particular slot machine for almost 48 hours when he realized that he was down to his last twenty dollars. With a potential one million dollar jackpot, he had no doubt what-so-ever that the slot machine was hot and ready to pay. With his last twenty dollars in hand, Jimmy took notice of two gentlemen standing next to him. Aware of his obvious dilemma, one of the gentlemen introduced himself and said, *"Sir, my friend and I have noticed that you have been on this machine for quite some time and we'd like to propose a partnership."*

Jimmy asked, *"What sort of partnership are you suggesting?"*

The gentleman replied, *"My friend and I believe there's a pretty good chance that this machine is about to pay the big jackpot and the two of us would be willing to keep you supplied with all the quarters you need to keep going, if in return you would be willing to split the jackpot evenly amongst the three of us."*

The offer was tempting, but Jimmy couldn't help but think to himself that he had already spent almost two days and close to a thousand dollars priming this machine for the big pay-off. He thought to himself, *I'm the one who's put all the time and money getting this machine hot! If these guys spend only $50 and I hit the jackpot, it wouldn't be fair that I have to split the money 3 ways!*

After a moment of consideration, Jimmy politely refused their offer and watched as the two gentlemen walked away most likely in search of another prospect.

Within 45 minutes, Jimmy had exhausted his last twenty dollars. Still convinced that the machine was close to a jackpot pay-out and regretting his decision, he sat looking around for the two gentlemen. Thirty minutes passed without a glimpse of the gentlemen, so Jimmy left the machine and went to his room for a much needed nap. During the two hours Jimmy lay sleeping, three different individuals played his machine. The 3rd person hit the one million dollar jackpot. Can you guess who supplied the quarters for this 3rd person?

The moral of the story is; don't be greedy! Jimmy would've been better to have accepted a three-way split of the jackpot. His greed left him with nothing while the two gentlemen went on to find someone else to help; someone who didn't mind sharing. Don't be so arrogant as to think that you are the only opportunity for someone else just because you have an ingenious idea or concept that they are interested in.

Jimmy was so consumed with how much time and money *he* had invested in the slot machine, that he failed to realize that without *his* investment of time and money, the machine wouldn't have been hot and therefore, worthy of the two gentlemen's financial contribution.

Most of the time, those that come into your life who can be instrumental in taking you and your ideas to the next level are not going to be concerned with the contribution you have made to get yourself to the point of their being interested. Don't take it personal! All that matters is that you have done what it takes to peak their interest. You don't need a pat on the back for what you have done; just accept their help and share the wealth if you believe they can take you to where you want to be. Let others help you till, sow, weed, water and wait!

You are going to want to attract those who will be willing to help you sow the seeds for your success, but in order to attract these people you will need to become a *money magnet*. This means you must read everything you can on how to obtain wealth, seek out those masters who have knowledge to share and be conscious of every dollar you spend and receive.

In 1955 a collection of the ancient laws of thrift and personal wealth was published in a book titled, *The Richest man in Babylon*. The 1st of the Babylonian secrets for achieving personal wealth was to, *Start thy purse to fattening*. The Babylonians believed in taking a portion of all one earned and claiming it as one's own. This portion was usually not less than 10 % and was kept in a purse worn at the waist. This was to act as a money magnet and as it grew fatter, they would transfer the excess to a larger box or use it for lending, buying property and making investments. They always kept a portion in their purse to attract more money. This exercise will be one of your seeds of action and believe me; it works!

Another important action for building wealth is to lessen what goes out while increasing what comes in. In the late 1990s, my wife and I began to analyze our financial situation. We realized that we were spending all of our energies trying to increase our in-coming flow of money to keep up with the constantly rising out-flow. We made a decision to find a way of decreasing what we spent without giving up our desired lifestyle.

Within two months of putting our heads together, we had decreased our expenditures by $2400 a month without sacrificing any of the comforts we were accustomed to. We did this by changing our light bulbs to a slightly lower wattage, by purchasing a home with a lower mortgage payment and by paying bills on time to avoid late fees, among other things.

What good does it do to attract money if you consistently increase your need for it. Be responsible. True abundance comes when you know exactly what you want. If you do not know exactly what you want, then you are doomed to be unhappy no matter how much you accumulate. You won't be able to determine if and when you have become wealthy.

I'm going to suggest plenty of examples in this area. Just make sure you include all forms of wealth when placing your order with the universe. Be exact!

Seeds of Thought:
- *Imagine yourself having more money than you could ever spend. What good would you do for others?*
- *Think of yourself as a money magnet.*
- *Think like a potential lottery winner. In other words, what are you going to do when you receive the jackpot?*
- *Think of every dollar in your pocket as a seed and refer to them in such a way. You will be less likely to waist a seed on unfertile ground.*
- *Worry never paid the bills! Think to yourself; I have an abundance of money, I **am** wealthy.*
- *When you list your seeds of thought, list the key people in your life that you want to help you increase your flow of*

money. For instance; "My boss is giving me a raise. He wants to increase my wealth."
- *Think; "My wife is a valuable asset. She is increasing my wealth with her support."*
- *Name a person you have a business meeting with and think; "Bob is meeting with me because he wants to increase my wealth."*
- *Think; "I am preparing myself for the job/business I want for I may have to start tomorrow." Name the job or business you want then prepare yourself in expectation of receiving it.*

Seeds of Word:
- *To become; act as if. If you are training to be an attorney, go ahead and call yourself one when others inquire about your profession. People will think of you, talk to you and treat you like an attorney, giving power to your desire. Please don't practice without a license.*
- *Ask those who are where you want to be how they did it. Ask for help!*
- *Ask for everything you want. You might be surprised at what others will give you when asked. If you want to start a catering business, ask anyone who has the ability to help you. This may be knowledge, equipment or clients.*
- *Look in the mirror and affirm out loud your goals as if they have happened.*
- *If you make a verbal commitment or promise; keep it! It does not matter if you have a valid contract or not. Keep your word! This applies to verbal commitments with yourself and your invisible partner as well.*
- *Do the exercise at the beginning of the book and affirm your responsibility to all that transpires in your world in a committed voice.*

- *When you awake and before going to bed; read aloud from your want-pages. Update as necessary.*

Seeds of Action: In this area, get up and sow 3 seeds of action toward your desired goal or outcome. If you wish to open a shoe store, then do at least 3 actions a day to get you to that outcome.

- *Purchase and read magazines that share other peoples' success stories. A few would be: Inc. Magazine, Success Magazine, Network Marketing Magazine and Selling Power Magazine. Keep fresh success in the forefront of your brain. Write the name of the magazine and what articles were read as a seed of action for a given day.*
- *Read how-to and autobiographic books by the masters of the seed. I have already listed a few, but spend some time in the biography and self-help sections of your library or book store. There are thousands of great books in this field. You may write whatever amount you have read as one of your seeds of action for a given day.*
- *Carry yourself with a posture that says, "This way to success, follow me!" To become, act as if.*
- *Network. Actively pursue others who are already where you want to be or who can help you get to where you want to be.*
- *Be a generous giver. Tip like a wealthy person.*
- *Carry a 100 dollar bill (not in the form of 10s or 20s) in your pocket as a magnet to attract money. Remember the Babylonian story. If you are at a place in life where you can't spare the $100 without needing it immediately, then you may start with $20 and work your way up. I suggest that you replace the magnet money every once in a while with a fresh bill.*

- *Seek multiple streams of income. Sow your money as seeds that will grow to spawn still other seeds. Sow your money seeds to grow abundance.*
- *Take steps to become debt-free. Money seems to come when we least need it. Desperation causes worry and impatience which can lead to leaving money on the table when dealing with others.*

When greeting people, even those you do business with, try a hug instead of a handshake. This makes your visit more personal and where business associates are concerned, they are less likely to use negative aggression. You can stick with the handshake upon first meeting, but after that, give the hug a try.

Set your goal, place your *exact* order with the universe and sow the seeds. This is how it has been done by every successful person for thousands of years whether they knew it or not. Just make sure to maintain a balance of wealth and understand that if you seek wealth, it will seek you.

EXACTLY WHAT I WANT
Date: _____

WEALTH
(SOWING SEEDS OF FINANCIAL FREEDOM: DAY 1)
Date: _____

Seed of <u>Thought</u> I

Seed of <u>Thought</u> II

Seed of <u>Thought</u> III

Seed of <u>Word</u> I

Seed of <u>Word</u> II

Seed of <u>Word</u> III

Seed of <u>Action</u> I

Seed of <u>Action</u> II

Seed of <u>Action</u> III

"I water these seeds with <u>faith</u> and fertilize them with <u>expectation</u>!"
Weeds to Watch!

_____
_____
_____
_____

WEALTH
(SOWING SEEDS OF FINANCIAL FREEDOM: DAY 2)
Date: _____

Seed of Thought I

_____
_____

Seed of Thought II

_____
_____

Seed of Thought III

_____
_____

Seed of Word I

_____
_____

Seed of Word II

_____
_____

Seed of Word III

_____
_____

Seed of Action I

_____
_____

Seed of Action II

_____
_____

Seed of Action III

_____
_____

"I water these seeds with <u>faith</u> and fertilize them with <u>expectation</u>!"
Weeds to Watch!

_____
_____
_____
_____

WEALTH
(SOWING SEEDS OF FINANCIAL FREEDOM: DAY 3)
Date: _____

Seed of Thought I

_____
_____

Seed of Thought II

_____
_____

Seed of Thought III

_____
_____

Seed of Word I

_____
_____

Seed of Word II

_____
_____

Seed of Word III

_____
_____

Seed of Action I

_____
_____

Seed of Action II

_____
_____

Seed of Action III

_____
_____

"I water these seeds with <u>faith</u> and fertilize them with <u>expectation</u>!"
Weeds to Watch!

_____
_____
_____
_____

WEALTH
(SOWING SEEDS OF FINANCIAL FREEDOM: DAY 4)
Date: _____

Seed of <u>Thought</u> I

_____
_____

Seed of <u>Thought</u> II

_____
_____

Seed of <u>Thought</u> III

_____
_____

Seed of <u>Word</u> I

_____
_____

Seed of <u>Word</u> II

_____
_____

Seed of <u>Word</u> III

_____
_____

Seed of <u>Action</u> I

_____
_____

Seed of <u>Action</u> II

_____
_____

Seed of <u>Action</u> III

_____
_____

"I water these seeds with <u>faith</u> and fertilize them with <u>expectation</u>!"
Weeds to Watch!

_____
_____
_____
_____

WEALTH
(SOWING SEEDS OF FINANCIAL FREEDOM: DAY 5)
Date: _____

Seed of Thought I

_____
_____

Seed of Thought II

_____
_____

Seed of Thought III

_____
_____

Seed of Word I

_____
_____

Seed of Word II

_____
_____

Seed of Word III

_____
_____

Seed of Action I

_____
_____

Seed of Action II

_____
_____

Seed of Action III

_____
_____

"I water these seeds with <u>faith</u> and fertilize them with <u>expectation</u>!"
Weeds to Watch!

_____

_____

_____

_____

WEALTH
(SOWING SEEDS OF FINANCIAL FREEDOM: DAY 6)

Date: _____

Seed of Thought I

Seed of Thought II

Seed of Thought III

Seed of Word I

Seed of Word II

Seed of Word III

Seed of Action I

Seed of Action II

Seed of Action III

"I water these seeds with <u>faith</u> and fertilize them with <u>expectation</u>!"
Weeds to Watch!

_____
_____
_____
_____

HARVEST: DAY 7
Date: _____

COMMUNITY

The number one rule here is to get involved! Go back to the section where I shared the examples of the masters. All *true* masters of the seed give back and get involved with their communities. They understand that it is the majority who lift the few to heights of success in this life. Churches, activists and non-profit organizations tend to serve their communities well. If you don't yet have a passion that benefits your neighbors, get involved and support someone else's cause.

When I make reference to *the community,* I'm referring to the *world* community and not just your local one. Getting involved and making a difference will serve to make you feel worthy of your successes elsewhere and will bring forth a harvest unlike all others. We all depend on our communities in some way or another, so we must support them. Take a look around and really take the time to absorb the impact of the different organizations on you, your business and your family. There are schools, churches, social service programs, community events and fundraisers and even for-profit companies that inadvertently help you and your family whether you need it or not.

I have certainly found my passion to serve. I am co-founder of a non-profit foundation called, **THE STAF-FOUNDATION, INC.** (Serving The American Family), where we support other non-profit organizations. We help those who dedicate their talents and resources for the benefit of others. I especially take an interest where children may benefit.

I am also the founder of **OPERATION: S.O.S.** (Serving Our Soldiers). Operation S.O.S. is a project where we provide preventative healing using therapists, life coaches and comedic entertainment for soldiers, veterans and their families. A high percentage of soldiers do not seek psychological support after leaving combat due to a feeling of shame and not wanting to seem weak. We provide the support they need on compact disc so that they can get the help they need in private. This project supports the soldiers' families as well.

If you would like to find out more on these organizations and how to support them, you can e-mail me at *seedsofpurpose@myway.com*.

Take your community involvement seriously as you will reap many rewards for you and your family.

EXACTLY WHAT I WANT

Date: _____

SOWING SEEDS OF PURPOSE (HOW TO HARVEST A LIFE ABUNDANT)

_____
_____
_____

SOWING SEEDS IN
MY COMMUNITY: DAY 1
Date: _____
Seed of Thought I

_____
_____

Seed of Thought II

_____
_____

Seed of Thought III

_____
_____

Seed of Word I

_____
_____

Seed of Word II

_____
_____

Seed of Word III

_____
_____

Seed of Action I

_____
_____

Seed of Action II

_____
_____

Seed of Action III

_____
_____

"I water these seeds with <u>faith</u> and fertilize them with <u>expectation</u>!"
Weeds to Watch!

_____
_____
_____
_____

SOWING SEEDS IN MY COMMUNITY: DAY 2

Date: _____

Seed of <u>Thought</u> I

_____
_____

Seed of <u>Thought</u> II

_____
_____

Seed of <u>Thought</u> III

_____
_____

Seed of <u>Word</u> I

_____
_____

Seed of <u>Word</u> II

_____
_____

Seed of <u>Word</u> III

_____
_____

Seed of <u>Action</u> I

_____
_____

Seed of <u>Action</u> II

_____
_____

Seed of <u>Action</u> III

_____
_____

"I water these seeds with <u>faith</u> and fertilize them with <u>expectation</u>!"
Weeds to Watch!

_____
_____
_____
_____

SOWING SEEDS IN MY COMMUNITY: DAY 3

Date: _____

Seed of Thought I
_____
_____

Seed of Thought II
_____
_____

Seed of Thought III
_____
_____

Seed of Word I
_____
_____

Seed of Word II
_____
_____

Seed of Word III
_____
_____

Seed of Action I
_____
_____

Seed of Action II
_____
_____

Seed of Action III
_____
_____

"I water these seeds with <u>faith</u> and fertilize them with <u>expectation</u>!"
Weeds to Watch!

_____
_____
_____
_____

SOWING SEEDS IN MY COMMUNITY: DAY 4

Date: _____

Seed of <u>Thought</u> I

Seed of <u>Thought</u> II

Seed of <u>Thought</u> III

Seed of <u>Word</u> I

Seed of <u>Word</u> II

Seed of <u>Word</u> III

Seed of <u>Action</u> I

Seed of <u>Action</u> II

Seed of <u>Action</u> III

"I water these seeds with <u>faith</u> and fertilize them with <u>expectation</u>!"
Weeds to Watch!

_____
_____
_____
_____

SOWING SEEDS IN
MY COMMUNITY: DAY 5
Date: _____
Seed of <u>Thought</u> I

_____
_____

Seed of <u>Thought</u> II

_____
_____

Seed of <u>Thought</u> III

_____
_____

Seed of <u>Word</u> I

_____
_____

Seed of <u>Word</u> II

_____
_____

Seed of <u>Word</u> III

_____
_____

Seed of <u>Action</u> I

_____
_____

Seed of <u>Action</u> II

_____
_____

Seed of <u>Action</u> III

_____
_____

"I water these seeds with <u>faith</u> and fertilize them with <u>expectation</u>!"
Weeds to Watch!

_____
_____
_____
_____

SOWING SEEDS IN MY COMMUNITY: DAY 6

Date: _____

Seed of <u>Thought</u> I

_____
_____

Seed of <u>Thought</u> II

_____
_____

Seed of <u>Thought</u> III

_____
_____

Seed of <u>Word</u> I

_____
_____

Seed of <u>Word</u> II

_____
_____

Seed of <u>Word</u> III

_____
_____

Seed of <u>Action</u> I

_____
_____

Seed of <u>Action</u> II

_____
_____

Seed of <u>Action</u> III

_____
_____

"*I water these seeds with <u>faith</u> and fertilize them with <u>expectation</u>!*"
Weeds to Watch!

_____

_____

_____

_____

HARVEST: DAY 7
Date: _____

GET TO KNOW THE GARDENER

To thine own self be true.

Before you start sowing, I want you to take a moment or a couple of days if you need to and think about whom you *truly* are and whom you truly want to be. A popular exercise in leadership workshops is to have the participants write their eulogy. What usually happens is that everyone tends to write the ideal description of themselves.

What I think would be a useful exercise, would be for you to write an absolutely truthful eulogy depicting what individuals closest to you would *really* say about you. I don't mean what they would say at the funeral. It would be rude for your friends and loved ones to be brutally honest about you at your funeral. I want you to write what you think they would say about who you are 2 weeks *after* the funeral.

Be brutally honest when writing how you think they really feel and you will come face to face with the person that others live with daily. Read the eulogy out loud in front of a mirror and then, if you're satisfied with their view of you; good. If you're *not* happy with their view, then make notes beside everything you don't like and decide for yourself if you think this needs changing.

I'm including a eulogy page so you will be able to reference the changes you wish to make about yourself. This is your chance to work on becoming the person you would like to be. Remember, this exercise is for the purpose of helping you come to terms with how you have lived, worked and loved those in your life and to help you address changes you wish to make that maybe you might not have seen as clearly before. I'm also creating a page for you to write down every little detail about the person you *want* to be. In other words, describe the person you wish to become.

Law # 9: *Be honest with yourself.*

MY EULOGY BY OTHERS

THIS IS WHO I AM NOW

THIS IS WHO I WANT TO BE

I'M HERE SHOULD YOU NEED ME

Before I leave you with my final thought, I want to encourage you to contact me if you have or are a member of a book club. I will be happy to join you and your group in discussion of the *sowing seeds of purpose principals*.

E-mail me at: seedsofpurpose@myway.com or visit my blog at: www.seedsofpurpose.com.

Contact Elbert for:
- Public Speaking
- Team-building workshops
- 1 on 1 life coaching/in person or by phone
- Group life coaching
- Small business and corporate marketing consultation
- Image and media coaching

INSTRUCTIONS FOR LIFE

- *Take into account that great love and great achievements involve great risks.*
- *When you lose, don't lose the lesson.*
- *Follow the three R's:*
    Respect for self
    Respect for others
    Responsibility for all your actions
- *Remember that not getting what you want is sometimes a wonderful stroke of luck.*
- *Learn the rules so you know how to break them properly.*
- *When you realize you've made a mistake, take immediate steps to correct it.*
- *Spend some time alone every day.*
- *Remember that silence is sometimes the best answer.*
- *Live a good, honorable life. Then when you get older and think back, you'll be able to enjoy it a 2nd time.*
- *A loving atmosphere in your home is the foundation for your life.*
- *In disagreements with loved ones deal only with the current situation. Don't bring up the past*
- *Share your knowledge. It is a way to achieve immortality.*
- *Be gentle with the earth.*
- *Once a year, go someplace you've never been before.*
- *Remember that the best relationship is one in which your love for each other exceeds your need for each other.*

- *Judge your success by what you had to give up in order to get it.*
- *Approach love and cooking with reckless abandon.*
- *Always be a class act!*

Author unknown

Law # 10: *Invite others to share your harvest and they will.*

Made in the USA